Travel phrasebooks collection
«Everything Will Be Okay!»

I0158337

PHRASEBOOK

THAI

THE MOST IMPORTANT PHRASES

This phrasebook contains the most important phrases and questions for basic communication
Everything you need to survive overseas

By Andrey Taranov

T&P BOOKS

Phrasebook + 1500-word dictionary

English-Thai phrasebook & concise dictionary

By Andrey Taranov

The collection of "Everything Will Be Okay" travel phrasebooks published by T&P Books is designed for people traveling abroad for tourism and business. The phrasebooks contain what matters most - the essentials for basic communication. This is an indispensable set of phrases to "survive" while abroad.

Another section of the book also provides a small dictionary with more than 1,500 useful words arranged alphabetically. The dictionary includes a lot of gastronomic terms and will be helpful when ordering food at a restaurant or buying groceries at the store.

Copyright © 2019 T&P Books Publishing

All rights reserved. No part of this book may be reproduced or utilized in any form or by any means, electronic or mechanical, including photocopying, recording or by information storage and retrieval system, without permission in writing from the publishers.

T&P Books Publishing
www.tpbooks.com

ISBN: 978-1-83955-081-2

This book is also available in E-book formats.
Please visit www.tpbooks.com or the major online bookstores.

FOREWORD

The collection of "Everything Will Be Okay" travel phrasebooks published by T&P Books is designed for people traveling abroad for tourism and business. The phrasebooks contain what matters most - the essentials for basic communication. This is an indispensable set of phrases to "survive" while abroad.

This phrasebook will help you in most cases where you need to ask something, get directions, find out how much something costs, etc. It can also resolve difficult communication situations where gestures just won't help.

This book contains a lot of phrases that have been grouped according to the most relevant topics. A separate section of the book also provides a small dictionary with more than 1,500 important and useful words.

Take "Everything Will Be Okay" phrasebook with you on the road and you'll have an irreplaceable traveling companion who will help you find your way out of any situation and teach you to not fear speaking with foreigners.

TABLE OF CONTENTS

T&P Books Publishing

PRONUNCIATION

T&P phonetic alphabet	Thai example	English example

Vowels

[a]	ห้า [hâ:] – hâa	shorter than in ask
[e]	เป็นลม [pen lom] – bpen lom	elm, medal
[i]	วินัย [wíʔ naj] – wí–nai	shorter than in feet
[o]	โกน [ko:n] – gohn	pod, John
[u]	ขุ่นเคือง [kʰùn kʰɯ:aŋ] – khùn kheuang	book
[aa]	ราคา [ra: kʰa:] – raa–khaa	calf, palm
[oo]	ภูมิใจ [pʰu:m tɕaj] – phoom jai	pool, room
[ee]	บัญชี [ban tɕʰi:] – ban–chee	feet, meter
[ɯ]	เดือน [dɯ:an] – deuan	similar to a longue schwa sound
[ɤ]	เงิน [ŋɤn] – ngern	e in "the"
[ae]	แปล [plɛ:] – bplae	longer than bed, fell
[ay]	เลข [lê:k] – lâyk	longer than in bell
[ai]	ไปป์ [paj] – bpai	time, white
[oi]	โพย [pʰo:j] – phoi	oil, boy, point
[ya]	สัญญา [sǎn ja:] – sǎn–yaa	Kenya, piano
[ɤ:i]	อบเชย [ʔòp tɕʰɤ:j] – òp–choie	Combination [ə:i]
[i:a]	หน้าเชียว [nâ: si:aw] – nâa sieow	year, here

Initial consonant sounds

[b]	บาง [ba:ŋ] – baang	baby, book
[d]	สีแดง [sǐ: dɛ:ŋ] – sěe daeng	day, doctor
[f]	มันฝรั่ง [man fà ràŋ] – man fà–ràng	face, food
[h]	เฮลซิงกิ [he:n siŋ kìʔ] – hayn–sing–gì	home, have
[y]	ยี่สิบ [jì: sìp] – yêe sìp	yes, New York
[g]	กรง [kroŋ] – grorng	game, gold
[kh]	เลขา [le: kʰǎ:] – lay–khǎa	work hard
[l]	เล็ก [lék] – lék	lace, people
[m]	เมลอน [me: lɔ:n] – may–lorn	magic, milk
[n]	หนัง [nǎŋ] – nǎng	name, normal
[ng]	เงือก [ŋɯ:ak] – ngêuak	English, ring
[bp]	เป็น [pen] – bpen	pencil, private
[ph]	เผา [pʰàw] – phào	top hat

T&P phonetic alphabet	Thai example	English example
[r]	เบอร์รี่ [bɤː rîː] – ber–rêe	rice, radio
[s]	ซ่อน [sôn] – sôrn	city, boss
[dt]	ดนตรี [don triː] – don–dtree	tourist, trip
[j]	ปั้นจั่น [pân tɕàn] – bpân jàn	cheer
[ch]	วิชา [wíʔ tɕʰaː] – wí–chaa	hitchhiker
[th]	แถว [tʰɛːw] – thǎe	don't have
[w]	เคียว [kʰǐːaw] – khieow	vase, winter

Final consonant sounds

[k]	แม่เหล็ก [mɛː lèk] – mâe lèk	clock, kiss
[m]	เพิ่ม [pʰɤːm] – phêrm	magic, milk
[n]	เนียน [niːan] – nian	name, normal
[ng]	เป็นห่วง [pen hùːaŋ] – bpen hùang	English, ring
[p]	ไม่ขยับ [mâj kʰà ja p] – mâi khà–yàp	pencil, private
[t]	ลูกเป็ด [lûːk pèt] – lôok bpèt	tourist, trip

Comments

˙ **Mid tone - [ā]** การคูณ [gaan khon]
Low tone - [à] แจกจ่าย [jàek jàai]
Falling tone - [â] แต่ม [dtâem]
High tone - [á] แซ็กโซโฟน [sáek-soh-fohn]
Rising tone - [ǎ] เนินเขา [nern khǎo]

LIST OF ABBREVIATIONS

English abbreviations

ab.	-	about
adj	-	adjective
adv	-	adverb
anim.	-	animate
as adj	-	attributive noun used as adjective
e.g.	-	for example
etc.	-	et cetera
fam.	-	familiar
fem.	-	feminine
form.	-	formal
inanim.	-	inanimate
masc.	-	masculine
math	-	mathematics
mil.	-	military
n	-	noun
pl	-	plural
pron.	-	pronoun
sb	-	somebody
sing.	-	singular
sth	-	something
v aux	-	auxiliary verb
vi	-	intransitive verb
vi, vt	-	intransitive, transitive verb
vt	-	transitive verb

T&P BOOKS

THAI
PHRASEBOOK

This section contains
important phrases that may
come in handy in various
real-life situations.
The phrasebook will help
you ask for directions, clarify
a price, buy tickets, and
order food at a restaurant

T&P Books Publishing

PHRASEBOOK
CONTENTS

T&P Books Publishing

The bare minimum

Excuse me, ...	ขอโทษครับ /ค่ะ/ khŏr thôht khráp /khâ/
Hello.	สวัสดีครับ /สวัสดีค่ะ/ sà-wàt-dee khráp /sà-wàt-dee khâ/
Thank you.	ขอบคุณครับ /ค่ะ/ khòrp khun khráp /khâ/
Good bye.	สวัสดีครับ /สวัสดีค่ะ/ sà-wàt-dee khráp /sà-wàt-dee khâ/
Yes.	ใช่ châi
No.	ไม่ใช่ mâi châi
I don't know.	ผม /ฉัน/ ไม่ทราบ phŏm /chăn/ mâi-sâap
Where? | Where to? | When?	ที่ไหน | ไปที่ไหน | เมื่อไหร่ thêe năi | bpai thêe năi | mêua rài

---

I need ...	ผม /ฉัน/ ต้องการ... phŏm /chăn/ dtôrng gaan...
I want ...	ผม /ฉัน/ ต้องการ... phŏm /chăn/ dtôrng gaan...
Do you have ...?	คุณมี...ไหมครับ /ค่ะ/ khun mee...măi khráp /khá/
Is there a ... here?	ที่นี่มี...ไหม thêe nêe mee...măi
May I ...?	ผม /ฉัน/ ขออนุญาต... phŏm /chăn/ khŏr a-nú-yâat...
..., please (polite request)	โปรด... bpròht...

I'm looking for ...	ผม /ฉัน/ กำลังหา... phŏm /chăn/ gam-lang hăa...
the restroom	ห้องน้ำ hôrng náam
an ATM	เอทีเอ็ม ay thee em
a pharmacy (drugstore)	ร้านขายยา ráan khăai yaa
a hospital	โรงพยาบาล rohng phá-yaa-baan
the police station	สถานีตำรวจ sà-thăa-nee dtam-rùat
the subway	รถไฟใต้ดิน rót fai dtâi din

a taxi	รถแท็กซี่
	rót tháek-sêe
the train station	สถานีรถไฟ
	sà-thăa-nee rót fai

My name is …	ผม /ฉัน/ ชื่อ...
	phŏm /chăn/ chêu…
What's your name?	คุณชื่ออะไรครับ /คะ/
	khun chêu a-rai khráp /khá/
Could you please help me?	ขอช่วยผมหน่อยครับ
	/ขอช่วยฉันหน่อยคะ/
	khŏr chûay phŏm nòi khráp
	/khŏr chûay chăn nòi khá/

I've got a problem.	ผม /ฉัน/ มีปัญหา
	phŏm /chăn/ mee bpan-hăa
I don't feel well.	ผม /ฉัน/ รู้สึกไม่สบาย
	phŏm /chăn/ róo sèuk mâi sà-baai
Call an ambulance!	ขอเรียกรถพยาบาล!
	khŏr rîak rót phá-yaa-baan
May I make a call?	ผม /ฉัน/ โทรศัพท์ได้ไหม
	phŏm /chăn/ thoh-rá-sàp dâai măi

I'm sorry.	ขอโทษ
	khŏr thôht
You're welcome.	ไม่เป็นไรครับ /ค่ะ/
	mâi bpen rai khráp /khâ/

I, me	ผม /ฉัน/
	phŏm /chăn/
you (inform.)	คุณ
	khun
he	เขา
	khăo
she	เธอ
	ther
they (masc.)	พวกเขา
	phûak khăo
they (fem.)	พวกเขา
	phûak khăo
we	เรา
	rao
you (pl)	คุณทั้งหลาย
	khun tháng lăai
you (sg, form.)	ท่าน
	thân

ENTRANCE	ทางเข้า
	thaang khâo
EXIT	ทางออก
	thaang òrk
OUT OF ORDER	เสีย
	sĭa

CLOSED	ปิด
	bpìt
OPEN	เปิด
	bpèrt
FOR WOMEN	สำหรับผู้หญิง
	sǎm-ràp phôo yǐng
FOR MEN	สำหรับผู้ชาย
	sǎm-ràp phôo chaai

Questions

Where?	ที่ไหน thêe năi
Where to?	ไปที่ไหน bpai thêe năi
Where from?	มาจากไหน maa jàak năi
Why?	ทำไม tham-mai
For what reason?	ด้วยเหตุผลอะไร dûay hàyt phŏn a-rai
When?	เมื่อไหร่ mêua rài

How long?	นานแค่ไหน naan khâe năi
At what time?	กี่โมง gèe mohng
How much?	ราคาเท่าไหร่ raa-khaa thâo rài
Do you have ...?	คุณมี...ไหมครับ /คะ/ khun mee…măi khráp /khá/
Where is ...?	...อยู่ที่ไหน …yòo thêe năi

What time is it?	กี่โมงแล้ว gèe mohng láew
May I make a call?	ผม /ฉัน/ โทรศัพท์ได้ไหม phŏm /chăn/ thoh-rá-sàp dâai măi
Who's there?	ใครอยู่ที่นั่น khrai yòo thêe nân
Can I smoke here?	ผม /ฉัน/ สูบบุหรี่ที่นี่ได้ไหม phŏm /chăn/ sòop bù rèe thêe nêe dâai măi
May I ...?	ผม /ฉัน/... ได้ไหม phŏm /chăn/… dâai măi

Needs

I'd like …	ผม /ฉัน/ ต้องการ phŏm /chăn/ dtôrng gaan
I don't want …	ผม /ฉัน/ ไม่ต้องการ phŏm /chăn/ mâi dtôrng gaan
I'm thirsty.	ผม /ฉัน/ หิวน้ำ phŏm /chăn/ hĭw náam
I want to sleep.	ผม /ฉัน/ ต้องการนอน phŏm /chăn/ dtônrg gaan norn

I want …	ผม /ฉัน/ ต้องการ… phŏm /chăn/ dtôrng gaan…
to wash up	ล้างหน้า láang nâa
to brush my teeth	แปรงฟัน bpraeng fan
to rest a while	พักนิดหน่อย phák nít nòi
to change my clothes	เปลี่ยนเสื้อผ้า bplìan sêua phâa

to go back to the hotel	กลับไปที่โรงแรม glàp bpai thêe rohng raem
to buy …	ซื้อ… séu…
to go to …	ไป… bpai…
to visit …	ไปเยี่ยม… bpai yîam…
to meet with …	พบกับ… phóp gàp…
to make a call	โทรศัพท์ thoh-rá-sàp

I'm tired.	ผม /ฉัน/ เหนื่อย phŏm /chăn/ nèuay
We are tired.	เราเหนื่อย rao nèuay
I'm cold.	ผม /ฉัน/ หนาว phŏm /chăn/ năao
I'm hot.	ผม /ฉัน/ ร้อน phŏm /chăn/ rórn
I'm OK.	ผม /ฉัน/ โอเค phŏm /chăn/ oh khay

I need to make a call.

ผม /ฉัน/ ต้องการโทรศัพท์
phŏm /chǎn/ dtôrng gaan thoh-rá-sàp

I need to go to the restroom.

ผม /ฉัน/ ต้องการไปห้องน้ำ
phŏm /chǎn/
dtôrng gaan bpai hôrng náam

I have to go.

ผม /ฉัน/ ต้องไปแล้ว
phŏm /chǎn/ dtôrng bpai láew

I have to go now.

ตอนนี้ผม /ฉัน/ ต้องไปแล้ว
dton-née phŏm /chǎn/ dtôrng bpai láew

Asking for directions

Excuse me, …	ขอโทษครับ /ค่ะ/ khŏr thôht khráp /khâ/
Where is …?	…อยู่ที่ไหน …yòo thêe năi
Which way is …?	…ไปทางไหนครับ /คะ/ …bpai thaang năi khráp /khá/
Could you help me, please?	ขอช่วยผมหน่อยครับ /ขอช่วยฉันหน่อยค่ะ/ khŏr chûay phŏm nòi khráp /khŏr chûay chăn nòi khá/

I'm looking for …	ผม /ฉัน/ กำลังหา… phŏm /chăn/ gam-lang hăa…
I'm looking for the exit.	ผม /ฉัน/ กำลังหา ทางออกครับ /คะ/ phŏm /chăn/ gam-lang hăa thaang òrk khráp /khâ/
I'm going to …	ผม /ฉัน/ กำลังไป… phŏm /chăn/ gam-lang bpai…
Am I going the right way to …?	ผม /ฉัน/ ไป… ถูกไหม phŏm /chăn/ bpai… thòok măi

Is it far?	อยู่ไกลไหม yòo glai măi
Can I get there on foot?	ผม /ฉัน/ เดินไปที่นั่นได้ไหม phŏm /chăn/ dern bpai thêe nân dâai măi
Can you show me on the map?	ขอชี้…ในแผนที่ ให้ดูครับ /คะ/ khŏr chée…nai phăen thêe hâi doo khráp /khá/
Show me where we are right now.	ขอชี้…ว่าตอนนี้เรา อยู่ที่ไหนครับ /คะ/ khŏr chée…wâa dton-née rao yòo thêe năi khráp /khá/

Here	ที่นี่ thêe nêe
There	ที่นั่น thêe nân

This way	ทางนี้ thaang née
Turn right.	เลี้ยวขวา líeow khwăa

Turn left.	**เลี้ยวซ้าย** líeow sáai
first (second, third) turn	**การเลี้ยว แรก (ที่สอง, ที่สาม)** gaan líeow · râek (thêe sŏng, thêe săam)
to the right	**ไปทางขวา** bpai thaang khwăa
to the left	**ไปทางซ้าย** bpai thaang sáai
Go straight ahead.	**ไปตรง** bpai dtrong

Signs

WELCOME!	ยินดีต้อนรับ! yin dee dtôn ráp
ENTRANCE	ทางเข้า thaang khâo
EXIT	ทางออก thaang òrk

PUSH	ผลัก phlàk
PULL	ดึง deung
OPEN	เปิด bpèrt
CLOSED	ปิด bpìt

FOR WOMEN	สำหรับผู้หญิง sǎm-ràp phôo yǐng
FOR MEN	สำหรับผู้ชาย sǎm-ràp phôo chaai
GENTLEMEN, GENTS	สุภาพบุรุษ (ผู้ชาย) sù-phâap bù-rùt (phôo chaai)
WOMEN	สุภาพสตรี (ผู้หญิง) sù-phâap sàt-dtree (phôo yǐng)

DISCOUNTS	ลดราคา lót raa-khaa
SALE	ขายของลดราคา khǎai khǒrng lót raa-khaa
FREE	ฟรี free
NEW!	ใหม่! mài
ATTENTION!	โปรดทราบ! bpròht sâap

NO VACANCIES	ไม่ว่าง mâi wâang
RESERVED	จองแล้ว jorng láew
ADMINISTRATION	การบริหาร gaan bor-rí-hǎan
STAFF ONLY	เฉพาะพนักงาน chà-phór phá-nák ngaan

BEWARE OF THE DOG!	ระวังสุนัข! rá-wang sù-nák
NO SMOKING!	ห้ามสูบบุหรี่! hâam sòop bù rèe
DO NOT TOUCH!	ห้ามแตะ! hâam dtàe
DANGEROUS	อันตราย an-dtà-raai
DANGER	อันตราย an-dtà-raai
HIGH VOLTAGE	ไฟฟ้าแรงสูง fai fáa raeng sŏong
NO SWIMMING!	ห้ามว่ายน้ำ hâam wâai náam
OUT OF ORDER	เสีย sĭa
FLAMMABLE	อันตรายติดไฟ an-dtà-raai dtìt fai
FORBIDDEN	ห้าม hâam
NO TRESPASSING!	ห้ามบุกรุก! hâam bùk rúk
WET PAINT	สียังไม่แห้ง sĕe yang mâi hâeng
CLOSED FOR RENOVATIONS	ปิดปรับปรุง bpìt bpràp bprung
WORKS AHEAD	งานก่อสร้าง ngaan gòr sâang
DETOUR	ทางเบี่ยง thaang bìang

Transportation. General phrases

plane	เครื่องบิน khrêuang bin
train	รถไฟ rót fai
bus	รถเมล์ rót may
ferry	เรือข้ามฟาก reua khâam fâak
taxi	รถแท็กซี่ rót tháek-sêe
car	รถยนต์ rót yon

schedule	ตารางเวลา dtaa-raang way-laa
Where can I see the schedule?	ผม /ฉัน/ ดูตารางเวลาได้ที่ไหน phŏm /chăn/ doo dtaa-raang way-laa dâai thêe năi
workdays (weekdays)	วันทำงาน wan tham ngaan
weekends	วันหยุดสุดสัปดาห์ wan yùt sùt sàp-daa
holidays	วันหยุด wan yùt

DEPARTURE	ขาออก khăa òrk
ARRIVAL	ขาเข้า khăa khâo
DELAYED	ล่าช้า lâa cháa
CANCELLED	ยกเลิก yók lêrk

next (train, etc.)	ถัดไป thàt bpai
first	แรก râek
last	สุดท้าย sùt tháai

When is the next ...?	...เที่ยวถัดไปออกเมื่อไหร่
	...thîeow thàt bpai òk mêua rài
When is the first ...?	...เที่ยวแรกออกเมื่อไหร่
	...thîeow râek òrk mêua rài
When is the last ...?	...เที่ยวสุดท้ายออกเมื่อไหร่
	...thîeow sùt tháai òk mêua rài

transfer (change of trains, etc.)	การเปลี่ยนสาย
	gaan bplìan sǎai
to make a transfer	เปลี่ยนสาย
	bplìan sǎai
Do I need to make a transfer?	ผม /ฉัน/ ต้องเปลี่ยนสายไหม
	phǒm /chǎn/ dtôrng bplìan sǎai mǎi

Buying tickets

Where can I buy tickets?	ผม /ฉัน/ ซื้อตั๋วได้ที่ไหน phŏm /chăn/ séu dtŭa dâai thêe năi
ticket	ตั๋ว dtŭa
to buy a ticket	ซื้อตั๋ว séu dtŭa
ticket price	ราคาตั๋ว raa-khaa dtŭa
Where to?	ไปไหน bpai năi
To what station?	ไปสถานีไหน bpai sà-thăa-nee năi
I need ...	ผม /ฉัน/ ต้องการ... phŏm /chăn/ dtôrng gaan...
one ticket	ตั๋วหนึ่งใบ dtŭa nèung bai
two tickets	ตั๋วสองใบ dtŭa sŏng bai
three tickets	ตั๋วสามใบ dtŭa săam bai
one-way	เที่ยวเดียว thîeow dieow
round-trip	ไปกลับ bpai glàp
first class	ชั้นหนึ่ง chán nèung
second class	ชั้นสอง chán sŏng
today	วันนี้ wan née
tomorrow	พรุ่งนี้ phrûng-née
the day after tomorrow	มะรืน má-reun
in the morning	ตอนเช้า dtorn-cháo
in the afternoon	ตอนบ่าย dtorn-bàai
in the evening	ตอนเย็น dtorn-yen

aisle seat	ที่นั่งติดทางเดิน
	thêe nâng dtìt thaang dern
window seat	ที่นั่งติดหน้าต่าง
	thêe nâng dtìt nâa dtàang
How much?	ราคาเท่าไหร่
	raa-khaa thâo rài
Can I pay by credit card?	ผม /ฉัน/
	จ่ายด้วยบัตรเครดิตได้ไหม
	phǒm /chǎn/
	jàai dûay bàt khray-dìt dâai mǎi

Bus

bus	รถเมล์
	rót may
intercity bus	รถเมล์วิ่งระหว่างเมือง
	rót may wîng rá-wàang meuang
bus stop	ป้ายรถเมล์
	bpâai rót may
Where's the nearest bus stop?	ป้ายรถเมล์ที่ใกล้ที่สุดอยู่ที่ไหน
	bpâai rót may thêe glâi thêe sùt yòo thêe nǎi
number (bus ~, etc.)	หมายเลข
	mǎai lâyk
Which bus do I take to get to …?	ผม /ฉัน/ ควรนั่งรถเมล์สายไหนที่จะไป…
	phǒm /chǎn/ khuan nâng rót may sǎai nǎi thêe jà bpai…
Does this bus go to …?	รถเมล์สายนี้ไป…หรือไม่
	rót may sǎai née bpai…rěu mâi
How frequent are the buses?	รถเมล์มาบ่อยแค่ไหน
	rót may maa bòi khâe nǎi

every 15 minutes	ทุก 15 นาที
	thúk sìp hâa · naa-thee
every half hour	ทุกครึ่งชั่วโมง
	thúk khrêung chûa mohng
every hour	ทุกชั่วโมง
	thúk chûa mohng
several times a day	วันละหลายครั้ง
	wan lá lǎai khráng
… times a day	วันละ…ครั้ง
	wan lá…khráng

schedule	ตารางเวลา
	dtaa-raang way-laa
Where can I see the schedule?	ผม /ฉัน/ ดูตารางเวลาได้ที่ไหน
	phǒm /chǎn/ doo dtaa-raang way-laa dâai thêe nǎi
When is the next bus?	รถเมล์ถัดไปมาเมื่อไหร่
	rót may thàt bpai maa mêua rài
When is the first bus?	รถเมล์แรกออกเมื่อไหร่
	rót may râek òk mêua rài
When is the last bus?	รถเมล์สุดท้ายออกเมื่อไหร่
	rót may sùt tháai òrk mêua rài

stop	ป้าย
	bpâai
next stop	ป้ายหน้า
	bpâai nâa
last stop (terminus)	ป้ายสุดท้าย
	bpâai sùt tháai
Stop here, please.	กรุณาจอดที่นี่ครับ /ค่ะ/
	gà-rú-naa jòrt thêe nêe khráp /khâ/
Excuse me, this is my stop.	ขอโทษ ผม /ฉัน/
	ขอลงป้ายนี้ครับ /คะ/
	khŏr thôht · phŏm /chăn/
	khŏr long bpâai née khráp /khâ/

Train

train	รถไฟ rót fai
suburban train	รถไฟชานเมือง rót fai chaan meuang
long-distance train	รถไฟทางไกล rót fai thaang glai
train station	สถานีรถไฟ sà-thǎa-nee rót fai
Excuse me, where is the exit to the platform?	ขอโทษ ทางออกไปยัง ชานชาลาอยู่ที่ไหน khǒr thôht thaang òrk bpai yang chaan chaa-laa yòo thêe nǎi
Does this train go to …?	รถไฟนี้ไป...ไหม rót fai née bpai…mǎi
next train	รถไฟขบวนถัดไป rót fai khà-buan thàt bpai
When is the next train?	รถไฟขบวนถัดไปมาเมื่อไหร่ rót fai khà-buan thàt bpai maa mêua rài
Where can I see the schedule?	ผม /ฉัน/ ดูตาราง เวลาได้ที่ไหน phǒm /chǎn/ doo dtaa-raang way-laa dâai thêe nǎi
From which platform?	จากชานชาลาไหน jàak chaan chaa-laa nǎi
When does the train arrive in …?	รถไฟมาถึง...เมื่อไหร่ rót fai maa thěung…mêua rài
Please help me.	กรุณาช่วยผม /ฉัน/ gà-rú-naa chûay phǒm /chǎn/
I'm looking for my seat.	ผม /ฉัน/ กำลังหา ที่นั่งของผม /ฉัน/ phǒm /chǎn/ gam-lang hǎa thêe nâng khǒrng phǒm /chǎn/
We're looking for our seats.	เรากำลังหาที่นั่งของเรา rao gam-lang hǎa thêe nâng khǒrng rao
My seat is taken.	มีคนเอาที่นั่ง ของผม /ฉัน/ แล้ว mee khon ao thêe nâng khǒrng phǒm /chǎn/ láew
Our seats are taken.	มีคนเอาที่นั่งของเราแล้ว mee khon ao thêe nâng khǒrng rao láew

I'm sorry but this is my seat.

ขอโทษ แต่นี่คือที่นั่ง
ของผม /ฉัน/
khŏr thôht · dtàe nêe kheu thêe nâng
khŏrng phŏm /chăn/

Is this seat taken?

มีคนนั่งที่นี่ไหม
mee khon nâng thêe nêe măi

May I sit here?

ผม /ฉัน/ นั่งที่นี้ได้ไหม
phŏm /chăn/ nâng thêe née dâai măi

On the train. Dialogue (No ticket)

Ticket, please.
ขอดูตั๋วครับ /ค่ะ/
khŏr doo dtŭa khráp /khâ/

I don't have a ticket.
ผม /ฉัน/ ไม่มีตั๋ว
phŏm /chăn/ mâi mee dtŭa

I lost my ticket.
ผม /ฉัน/ ทำตั๋ว
ของผม /ฉัน/ หาย
phŏm /chăn/ tham dtŭa
khŏrng phŏm /chăn/ hăai

I forgot my ticket at home.
ผม /ฉัน/ ลืมตั๋วของผม
/ฉัน/ ไว้ที่บ้าน
phŏm /chăn/ leum dtŭa khŏrng phŏm
/chăn/ wái thêe bâan

You can buy a ticket from me.
คุณซื้อตั๋วได้ที่ผมได้ครับ
/ คุณซื้อตั๋วได้ที่ฉันได้คะ
khun séu dtŭa thêe phŏm dâai khráp
/ khun séu dtŭa thêe chăn dâai khâ

You will also have to pay a fine.
คุณยังต้องจ่ายค่าปรับด้วย
khun yang dtôrng jàai khâa bpràp dûay

Okay.
โอเค
oh khay

Where are you going?
คุณไปไหน
khun bpai năi

I'm going to …
ผม /ฉัน/ กำลังไป
phŏm /chăn/ gam-lang bpai

How much? I don't understand.
เท่าไหร่ ผม /ฉัน/ ไม่เข้าใจ
thâo rài · phŏm /chăn/ mâi khâo jai

Write it down, please.
กรุณาเขียนให้ดูครับ /ค่ะ/
gà-rú-naa khĭan hâi doo khráp /khâ/

Okay. Can I pay with a credit card?
โอเค. ผม /ฉัน/
จ่ายด้วยบัตรเครดิตได้ไหม
oh khay · phŏm /chăn/
jàai dûay bàt khray-dìt dâai măi

Yes, you can.
ได้ครับ /ค่ะ/
dâai khráp /khâ/

Here's your receipt.
นี่คือใบเสร็จของคุณครับ /ค่ะ/
nêe kheu bai sèt khŏrng khun khráp /khâ/

Sorry about the fine.
เสียใจด้วยค่าปรับ
sĭa jai dûay khâa bpràp

That's okay. It was my fault.

**ไม่เป็นไรหรอก เป็นความผิด
ของผม /ฉัน/ เอง**
mâi bpen rai ròk · bpen khwaam phìt
khŏrng phŏm /chăn/ ayng

Enjoy your trip.

ขอให้เที่ยวให้สนุกครับ /ค่ะ/
khŏr hâi thîeow hâi sà-nùk khráp /khâ/

Taxi

taxi	รถแท็กซี่ rót tháek-sêe
taxi driver	คนขับรถแท็กซี่ khon khàp rót tháek-sêe
to catch a taxi	เรียกรถแท็กซี่ rîak rót táek-sêe
taxi stand	ที่จอดรถแท็กซี่ thêe jòrt rót tháek sêe
Where can I get a taxi?	ผม /ฉัน/ เอารถแท็กซี่ได้ที่ไหน phǒm /chǎn/ ao rót tháek-sêe dâai thêe nǎi
to call a taxi	เรียกรถแท็กซี่ rîak rót táek-sêe
I need a taxi.	ผม /ฉัน/ ต้องการเรียกรถแท็กซี่ phǒm /chǎn/ dtôrng gaan rîak rót tháek-sêe
Right now.	ตอนนี้ dtorn-née
What is your address (location)?	ที่อยู่ของคุณคืออะไร thêe yòo khǒrng khun kheu a-rai
My address is …	ที่อยู่ของผม /ฉัน/ คือ... thêe yòo khǒrng phǒm /chǎn/ kheu...
Your destination?	คุณไปที่ไหน khun bpai thêe nǎi
Excuse me, …	ขอโทษครับ /ค่ะ/ khǒr thôht khráp /khâ/
Are you available?	คุณว่างไหมครับ /ค่ะ/ khun wâang mǎi khráp /khá/
How much is it to get to …?	ไป...ราคาเท่าไหร่ bpai...raa-khaa thâo rài
Do you know where it is?	คุณรู้ไหมว่ามันอยู่ที่ไหน ครับ /ค่ะ/ khun róo mǎi wâa man yòo thêe nǎi khráp /khá/
Airport, please.	ไปสนามบินครับ /ค่ะ/ bpai sà-nǎam bin khráp /khâ/
Stop here, please.	กรุณาจอดที่นี่ครับ /ค่ะ/ gà-rú-naa jòrt thêe nêe khráp /khâ/
It's not here.	ไม่ใช่ที่นี่ mâi châi thêe nêe

This is the wrong address.	ที่อยู่นี้ผิด
	thêe yòo née phìt
Turn left.	เลี้ยวซ้าย
	líeow sáai
Turn right.	เลี้ยวขวา
	líeow khwǎa

How much do I owe you?	ผม /ฉัน/ ต้องจ่ายเท่าไร
	phǒm /chǎn/ dtôrng jàai thâo rai
I'd like a receipt, please.	ขอใบเสร็จครับ /ค่ะ/
	khǒr bai sèt khráp /khâ/
Keep the change.	เก็บเงินทอนไว้เถอะ
	gèp ngern thorn wái thùh

Would you please wait for me?	ขอรอผมครับ /ฉันคะ/
	khǒr ror phǒm khráp /chǎn khá/
five minutes	ห้านาที
	hâa naa-thee
ten minutes	สิบนาที
	sìp naa-thee
fifteen minutes	สิบห้านาที
	sìp hâa naa-thee
twenty minutes	ยี่สิบนาที
	yêe sìp naa-thee
half an hour	ครึ่งชั่วโมง
	khrêung chûa mohng

Hotel

Hello.	สวัสดีครับ /ค่ะ/ sà-wàt-dee khráp /khâ/
My name is …	ผม /ฉัน/ ชื่อ… phŏm /chǎn/ chêu…
I have a reservation.	ผม /ฉัน/ ได้จองห้องไว้แล้ว phŏm /chǎn/ dâai jorng hôrng wái láew
I need …	ผม /ฉัน/ ต้องการ… phŏm /chǎn/ dtôrng gaan…
a single room	ห้องเตียงเดี่ยว hôrng dtiang dìeow
a double room	ห้องเตียงคู่ hôrng dtiang khôo
How much is that?	ราคาเท่าไหร่ raa-khaa thâo rài
That's a bit expensive.	ค่อนข้างแพง khôrn khâang phaeng
Do you have anything else?	คุณมีอะไรอย่างอื่นไหม ครับ /ค่ะ/ khun mee a-rai yàang èun măi khráp /khá/
I'll take it.	ผม /ฉัน/ จะเอาอันนี้ phŏm /chǎn/ jà ao an née
I'll pay in cash.	ผม /ฉัน/ จะจ่ายเป็นเงินสด phŏm /chǎn/ jà jàai bpen ngern sòt
I've got a problem.	ผม /ฉัน/ มีปัญหา phŏm /chǎn/ mee bpan-hăa
My … is broken.	…ของผม /ฉัน/ แตก …khŏng phŏm /chǎn/ dtàek
My … is out of order.	…ของผม /ฉัน/ เสีย …khŏng phŏm /chǎn/ sĭa
TV	โทรทัศน์ thoh-rá-thát
air conditioner	เครื่องปรับอากาศ khrêuang bpràp-aa-gàat
tap	ก๊อกน้ำ górk náam
shower	ฝักบัว fàk bua
sink	อ่างล้างหน้า àang láang-nâa

safe	ตู้เซฟ dtôo sâyf
door lock	กุญแจประตู gun-jae bprà-dtoo
electrical outlet	เต้าเสียบไฟฟ้า dtâo sìap fai fáa
hairdryer	ไดร์เป่าผม drai bpào phǒm
I don't have …	ผม /ฉัน/ ไม่มี... phǒm /chǎn/ mâi mee…
water	น้ำ náam
light	ไฟ fai
electricity	ไฟฟ้า fai fáa
Can you give me …?	คุณเอา...ให้ผม /ฉัน/ ได้ไหม ครับ /คะ/ khun au...hâi phǒm /chǎn/ dâai mǎi khráp /khá/
a towel	ผ้าเช็ดตัว phâa chét dtua
a blanket	ผ้าห่ม phâa hòm
slippers	รองเท้าแตะ rorng tháo dtàe
a robe	เสื้อคลุมอาบน้ำ sêua klum àap náam
shampoo	แชมพู chaem phoo
soap	สบู่ sà-bòo
I'd like to change rooms.	ผม /ฉัน/ ต้องการเปลี่ยนห้อง phǒm /chǎn/ dtôrng gaan bplìan hôrng
I can't find my key.	ผม /ฉัน/ หากุญแจไม่เจอ phǒm /chǎn/ hǎa gun-jae mâi jer
Could you open my room, please?	กรุณาช่วยเปิดห้อง ของผมครับ /ฉันคะ/ gà-rú-naa chûay bpèrt hôrng khǒrng phǒm khráp /chǎn khá/
Who's there?	**krai yòo têe nân** khrai yòo thêe nân
Come in!	เข้ามาครับ /ค่ะ/! khâo maa khráp /khâ/
Just a minute!	รอสักครู่! ror sàk khrôo
Not right now, please.	ไม่ใช่ตอนนี้ครับ /ค่ะ/ mâi châi dtorn-née khráp /khâ/

Come to my room, please.	กรุณามาที่ห้อง ของผมครับ /ฉันคะ/ gà-rú-naa maa thêe hôrng kŏrng phŏm khráp /chăn khâ/
I'd like to order food service.	ผม /ฉัน/ ต้องการสั่งอาหาร phŏm /chăn/ dtông gaan sàng aa-hăan
My room number is …	ห้องของผม /ฉัน/ มีเบอร์… hôrng kŏrng phŏm /chăn/ mee ber…

I'm leaving …	ผม /ฉัน/ กำลังออกไป… phŏm /chăn/ gam-lang òk bpai…
We're leaving …	พวกเรากำลังออกไป… phûak rao gam-lang òk bpai…
right now	ตอนนี้ dtorn-née
this afternoon	บ่ายนี้ bàai née
tonight	คืนนี้ kheun née
tomorrow	พรุ่งนี้ phrûng-née
tomorrow morning	พรุ่งนี้เวลาเช้า phrûng-née way-laa cháo
tomorrow evening	พรุ่งนี้เวลาเย็น phrûng-née way-laa yen
the day after tomorrow	มะรืน má-reun

I'd like to pay.	ผม /ฉัน/ ต้องการจ่าย phŏm /chăn/ dtông gaan jàai
Everything was wonderful.	ทุกอย่างดีเยี่ยม thúk yàang dee yîam
Where can I get a taxi?	ผม /ฉัน/ เรียกรถแท็กซี่ ได้ที่ไหน phŏm /chăn/ rîak rót tháek-sêe dâai thêe năi
Would you call a taxi for me, please?	กรุณาช่วยเรียกรถแท็ก ให้ผมครับ /ฉันคะ/ gà-rú-naa chûay rîak rót tháek-sêe hâi phŏm khráp /chăn khá/

Restaurant

Can I look at the menu, please?	ขอผม /ฉัน/ ดูเมนูหน่อย khŏr phŏm /chăn/ doo may-noo nòi
Table for one.	ขอโต๊ะสำหรับหนึ่งที่ khŏr dtó săm-ràp nèung thêe
There are two (three, four) of us.	เรามากันสอง (สาม สี่) คน rao maa gan sŏrng (săam · sèe) khon

Smoking	ห้องสูบบุหรี่ hôrng sòop bù rèe
No smoking	ห้องไม่สูบบุหรี่ hôrng mâi sòop bù rèe
Excuse me! (addressing a waiter)	ขอโทษครับ /ค่ะ/ khŏr thôht khráp /khâ/
menu	เมนู may-noo
wine list	รายการไวน์ raai gaan wai
The menu, please.	ขอเมนูด้วยครับ /ค่ะ/ khŏr may-noo dûay khráp /khâ/

Are you ready to order?	คุณพร้อมสั่งอาหารไหม ครับ /คะ/ khun phrórm sàng aa-hăan măi khráp /khá/
What will you have?	คุณต้องการอะไรบ้างครับ /คะ/ khun dtôrng gaan a-rai bâang khráp /khá/
I'll have …	ผม /ฉัน/ ต้องการ... phŏm /chăn/ dtôrng gaan…

I'm a vegetarian.	ผม /ฉัน/ กินมังสวิรัติ phŏm /chăn/ gin mang-sà-wí-rát
meat	เนื้อ néua
fish	ปลา bplaa
vegetables	ผัก phàk
Do you have vegetarian dishes?	คุณมีอาหารมังสวิรัติไหม ครับ /คะ/ khun mee aa hăan mang-sà-wí-rát măi khráp /khá/
I don't eat pork.	ผม /ฉัน/ ไม่กินเนื้อหมู phŏm /chăn/ mâi gin néua mŏo

He /she/ doesn't eat meat.	เขา /เธอ/ ไม่กินเนื้อสัตว์ khǎo /ther/ mâi gin néua sàt
I am allergic to …	ผม /ฉัน/ แพ้… phǒm /chǎn/ pháe…

Would you please bring me …	ขอเอา…ให้ผม /ฉัน/ khǒr ao…hâi phǒm /chǎn/
salt | pepper | sugar	เกลือ | พริกไทย | น้ำตาล gleua | phrík-tai | nám dtaan
coffee | tea | dessert	กาแฟ | ชา | ขนมหวาน gaa-fae | chaa | khà-nǒm wǎan
water | sparkling | plain	น้ำ | น้ำโซดา | น้ำเปล่า náam | náam soh-daa | náam bplào
a spoon | fork | knife	ช้อน | ส้อม | มีด chórn | sôrm | mêet
a plate | napkin	จาน | ผ้าเช็ดปาก jaan | phâa chét bpàak

Enjoy your meal!	ประทานอาหารให้อร่อยครับ /ค่ะ/! bprà-thaan aa-hǎan hâi a-ròi khráp /khâ/
One more, please.	ขออีกอันหนึ่งครับ /ค่ะ/ khǒr èek an nèung khráp /khâ/
It was very delicious.	อร่อยมาก a-ròi mâak

check | change | tip	คิดเงิน | เงินทอน | ทิป khít ngern | ngern thorn | thíp
Check, please. (Could I have the check, please?)	ขอคิดเงินครับ /ค่ะ/ khǒr khít ngern khráp /khâ/
Can I pay by credit card?	ผม /ฉัน/ จ่ายด้วย บัตรเครดิตได้ไหม phǒm /chǎn/ jàai dûay bàt khray-dìt dâai mǎi
I'm sorry, there's a mistake here.	ขอโทษ ตรงนี้มีข้อผิด khǒr thôht · dtrong née mee khôr phìt

Shopping

Can I help you?
ผม /ฉัน/ ช่วยคุณได้
ไหมครับ /คะ/
phǒm /chǎn/ chûay khun dâai
mǎi khráp /khá/

Do you have …?
คุณมี…ไหม
khun mee…mǎi

I'm looking for …
ผม /ฉัน/ กำลังหา…
phǒm /chǎn/ gam-lang hǎa…

I need …
ผม /ฉัน/ ต้องการ…
phǒm /chǎn/ dtôrng gaan…

I'm just looking.
ผม /ฉัน/ กำลังดูเท่านั้น
phǒm /chǎn/ gam-lang doo thâo nán

We're just looking.
พวกเรากำลังดูเท่านั้น
phûak rao gam-lang doo thâo nán

I'll come back later.
ผม /ฉัน/ จะกลับมาใหม่
phǒm /chǎn/ jà glàp maa mài

We'll come back later.
เราจะกลับมาใหม่
rao jà glàp maa mài

discounts | sale
ลดราคา | ขายของลดราคา
lót raa-khaa | khǎai khǒng lót raa-khaa

Would you please show me …
ผม /ฉัน/ ดู…ได้ไหม
phǒm /chǎn/ doo…dâai mǎi

Would you please give me …
ขอเอา…ให้ผม /ฉัน/
khǒr ao…hâi phǒm /chǎn/

Can I try it on?
ผม /ฉัน/ ลองได้ไหม
phǒm /chǎn/ lorng dâai mǎi

Excuse me, where's the fitting room?
ขอโทษ ห้องลองอยู่ที่ไหน
khǒr thôht hôrng lorng yòo thêe nǎi

Which color would you like?
คุณต้องการสีอะไร
khun dtôrng gaan sěe a-rai

size | length
ขนาด | ความยาว
khà-nàat | khwaam yaao

How does it fit?
พอดีไหม
phor dee mǎi

How much is it?
ราคาเท่าไหร่
raa-khaa thâo rài

That's too expensive.
แพงเกินไป
phaeng gern bpai

I'll take it.
ผม /ฉัน/ จะเอาอันนี้
phǒm /chǎn/ jà ao an née

Excuse me, where do I pay?	ขอโทษ ผม /ฉัน/ จ่ายเงินได้ที่ไหน khŏr thôht · phŏm /chăn/ jàai ngern dâai thêe năi
Will you pay in cash or credit card?	คุณจะจ่ายด้วยเงินสดหรือ บัตรเครดิต khun jà jàai dûay ngern sòt rĕu bàt khray-dìt
In cash | with credit card	เงินสด | บัตรเครดิต ngern sòt | bàt khray-dìt

Do you want the receipt?	คุณต้องการใบเสร็จไหม khun dtôrng gaan bai sèt măi
Yes, please.	ใช่ครับ /ค่ะ/ châi khráp /khâ/
No, it's OK.	ไม่ ไม่เป็นไร mâi · mâi bpen rai
Thank you. Have a nice day!	ขอบคุณครับ /ค่ะ/ ขอให้วันนี้เป็นวันที่ดีนะครับ /ค่ะ/ khòrp khun khráp /khâ/ khŏr hâi wan née bpen wan thêe dee ná khráp /khâ/

In town

Excuse me, …	ขอโทษครับ /ค่ะ/ khŏr thôht khráp /khâ/
I'm looking for …	ผม /ฉัน/ กำลังหา... phŏm /chăn/ gam-lang hăa…
the subway	รถไฟใต้ดิน rót fai dtâi din
my hotel	โรงแรมของผม /ฉัน/ rohng raem khŏrng phŏm /chăn/
the movie theater	โรงภาพยนตร์ rohng phâa-pha-yon
a taxi stand	จุดจอดแท็กซี่ jùt jòrt tháek-sêe
an ATM	เอทีเอ็ม ay thee em
a foreign exchange office	ที่แลกเงิน thêe lâek ngern
an internet café	ร้านอินเทอร์เนทคาเฟ่ ráan in thêr-nâyt kaa-fây
… street	ถนน... thà-nŏn…
this place	สถานที่นี้ sà-thăan thêe née
Do you know where … is?	คุณรู้ไหมว่า...อยู่ที่ไหน khun róo măi wâa…yòo thêe năi
Which street is this?	นี่คือถนนอะไร nêe kheu thà-nŏn a-rai
Show me where we are right now.	ขอชี้...ว่าตอนนี้เรา อยู่ที่ไหนครับ /ค่ะ/ khŏr chée…wâa dtorn-née rao yòo thêe năi khráp /khá/
Can I get there on foot?	ผม /ฉัน/ เดินไปได้ที่นั่นไหม phŏm /chăn/ dern bpai thêe nân dâai măi
Do you have a map of the city?	คุณมีแผนที่เมืองนี้ไหม khun mee phăen thêe meuang née măi
How much is a ticket to get in?	ตั๋วราคาเท่าไหร่ dtŭa raa-khaa thâo rài
Can I take pictures here?	ผม /ฉัน/ ถ่ายรูป ที่นี่ได้ไหม phŏm /chăn/ thàai rôop thêe nêe dâai măi

Are you open?	เปิดไหม bpèrt măi
When do you open?	คุณเปิดเมื่อไหร่ครับ /คะ/ khun bpèrt mêua rài khráp /khá/
When do you close?	คุณเปิดเมื่อไหร่ครับ /คะ/ khun bpìt mêua rài khráp /khá/

Money

money	เงิน ngern
cash	เงินสด ngern sòt
paper money	ธนบัตร thá-ná-bàt
loose change	เศษเหรียญ sàyt rĭan
check | change | tip	คิดเงิน | เงินทอน | ทิป khít ngern | ngern thorn | thíp
credit card	บัตรเครดิต bàt khray-dìt
wallet	กระเป๋าเงิน grà-bpǎo ngern
to buy	ซื้อ séu
to pay	จ่าย jàai
fine	ค่าปรับ khâa bpràp
free	ฟรี free
Where can I buy …?	ผม /ฉัน/ ซื้อ…ได้ที่ไหน phǒm /chǎn/ séu…dâai thêe nǎi
Is the bank open now?	ตอนนี้ธนาคารเปิดไหม dtorn-née thá-naa-khaan bpèrt mǎi
When does it open?	มันเปิดเมื่อไหร่ man bpèrt mêua rài
When does it close?	มันปิดเมื่อไหร่ man bpìt mêua rài
How much?	เท่าไหร่ thâo rài
How much is this?	อันนี้ราคาเท่าไหร่ an née raa-khaa thâo rài
That's too expensive.	แพงเกินไป phaeng gern bpai
Excuse me, where do I pay?	ขอโทษ ผม /ฉัน/ จ่ายเงินได้ที่ไหน khǒr thôht · phǒm /chǎn/ jàai ngern dâai thêe nǎi

Check, please.	ขอคิดเงินครับ /ค่ะ/ khŏr khít ngern khráp /khâ/
Can I pay by credit card?	ผม /ฉัน/ จ่ายด้วย บัตรเครดิตได้ไหม phŏm /chăn/ jàai dûay bàt khray-dìt dâai măi
Is there an ATM here?	ที่นี่มีตู้เอทีเอ็มไหม thêe nêe mee dtôo ay thee em măi
I'm looking for an ATM.	ผม /ฉัน/ กำลังหา ตู้เอทีเอ็ม phŏm /chăn/ gam-lang hăa dtôo ay thee em
I'm looking for a foreign exchange office.	ผม /ฉัน/ กำลังหา ที่แลกเงิน phŏm /chăn/ gam-lang hăa thêe lâek ngern
I'd like to change ...	ผม /ฉัน/ ต้องการแลก... phŏm /chăn/ dtôrng gaan lâek...
What is the exchange rate?	อัตราแลกเปลี่ยนเท่าไหร่ àt-dtraa lâek bplìan thâo rài
Do you need my passport?	คุณต้องการหนังสือเดินทาง ของผม /ฉัน/ ไหม khun dtôrng gaan năng-sĕu dern-thaang khŏrng phŏm /chăn/ măi

Time

What time is it?	กี่โมงแล้ว
	gèe mohng láew
When?	เมื่อไหร่
	mêua rài
At what time?	กี่โมง
	gèe mohng
now | later | after …	ตอนนี้ | ทีหลัง | หลังจาก...
	dtorn-née | thee lǎng | lǎng jàak…

one o'clock	หนึ่งนาฬิกา
	nèung naa-lí-gaa
one fifteen	หนึ่งนาฬิกาสิบห้านาที
	nèung naa-lí-gaa sìp hâa naa-thee
one thirty	หนึ่งนาฬิกาสามสิบนาที
	nèung naa-lí-gaa sǎam sìp naa-thee
one forty-five	หนึ่งนาฬิกาสี่สิบห้านาที
	nèung naa-lí-gaa sèe-sìp-hâa naa-thee

one | two | three	หนึ่ง | สอง | สาม
	nèung | sǒrng | sǎam
four | five | six	สี่ | ห้า | หก
	sèe | hâa | hòk
seven | eight | nine	เจ็ด | แปด | เก้า
	jèt | bpàet | gâo
ten | eleven | twelve	สิบ | สิบเอ็ด | สิบสอง
	sìp | sìp èt | sìp sǒrng

in …	อีก...
	èek…
five minutes	ห้านาที
	hâa naa-thee
ten minutes	สิบนาที
	sìp naa-thee
fifteen minutes	สิบห้านาที
	sìp hâa naa-thee
twenty minutes	ยี่สิบนาที
	yêe sìp naa-thee
half an hour	ครึ่งชั่วโมง
	khrêung chûa mohng
an hour	หนึ่งชั่วโมง
	nèung chûa mohng

in the morning	ตอนเช้า dtorn-cháo
early in the morning	แต่เช้า dtàe cháo
this morning	วันนี้เวลาเช้า wan née way-laa cháo
tomorrow morning	พรุ่งนี้เวลาเช้า phrûng-née way-laa cháo
in the middle of the day	กลางวัน glaang wan
in the afternoon	ตอนบ่าย dtorn-bàai
in the evening	ตอนเย็น dtorn-yen
tonight	คืนนี้ kheun née
at night	เที่ยงคืน thîang kheun
yesterday	เมื่อวานนี้ mêua waan née
today	วันนี้ wan née
tomorrow	พรุ่งนี้ phrûng-née
the day after tomorrow	มะรืน má-reun
What day is it today?	วันนี้คือวันอะไร wan née kheu wan a-rai
It's ...	วันนี้คือ... wan née kheu...
Monday	วันจันทร์ wan jan
Tuesday	วันอังคาร wan ang-khaan
Wednesday	วันพุธ wan phút
Thursday	วันพฤหัส wan phá-réu-hàt
Friday	วันศุกร์ wan sùk
Saturday	วันเสาร์ wan săo
Sunday	วันอาทิตย์ wan aa-thít

Greetings. Introductions

Hello.	สวัสดีครับ /ค่ะ/ sà-wàt-dee khráp /khâ/
Pleased to meet you.	ยินดีที่รู้จักครับ /ค่ะ/ yin dee thêe róo jàk khráp /khâ/
Me too.	เช่นกัน chên gan
I'd like you to meet …	ผม /ฉัน/ อยากให้คุณพบกับ… phǒm /chǎn/ yàak hâi khun phóp gàp…
Nice to meet you.	ยินดีที่รู้จักครับ /ค่ะ/ yin dee thêe róo jàk khráp /khâ/

How are you?	เป็นอย่างไรบ้าง bpen yàang rai bâang
My name is …	ผม /ฉัน/ ชื่อ… phǒm /chǎn/ chêu…
His name is …	เขาชื่อ… khǎo chêu…
Her name is …	เธอชื่อ… ther chêu…
What's your name?	คุณชื่ออะไร khun chêu a-rai
What's his name?	เขาชื่ออะไร khǎo chêu a-rai
What's her name?	เธอชื่ออะไร ther chêu a-rai

What's your last name?	นามสกุลของคุณคืออะไร naam sà-gun khǒrng khun kheu a-rai
You can call me …	คุณเรียกผมว่า…ก็ได้ ครับ /ค่ะ/ khun rîak phǒm wâa…gôr dâai khráp /khâ/
Where are you from?	คุณมาจากที่ไหนครับ /คะ/ khun maa jàak thêe nǎi khráp /khá/
I'm from …	ผม /ฉัน/ มาจาก… phǒm /chǎn/ maa jàak…
What do you do for a living?	คุณมีอาชีพอะไรครับ /คะ/ khun mee aa-chêep a-rai khráp /khá/

Who is this?	นี่คือใครครับ /คะ/ nêe kheu khrai khráp /khá/
Who is he?	เขาคือใคร khǎo kheu khrai

Who is she?	เธอคือใคร
	ther kheu khrai
Who are they?	พวกเขาคือใครครับ /คะ/
	phûak khǎo kheu khrai khráp /khá/

This is …	นี่คือ...ครับ /ค่ะ/
	nêe kheu…khráp /khâ/
my friend (masc.)	เพื่อนของผม /ฉัน/
	phêuan khǒrng phǒm /chǎn/
my friend (fem.)	เพื่อนของผม /ฉัน/
	phêuan khǒrng phǒm /chǎn/
my husband	สามีของฉัน
	sǎa-mee khǒrng chǎn
my wife	ภรรยาของผม
	phan-rá-yaa khǒrng phǒm

my father	พ่อของผม /ฉัน/
	phôr khǒrng phǒm /chǎn/
my mother	แม่ของผม /ฉัน/
	mâe khǒrng phǒm /chǎn/
my brother	พี่ชายของผม /ฉัน/,
	น้องชายของผม /ฉัน/
	phêe chaai khǒrng phǒm /chǎn/,
	nóng chaai khǒrng phǒm /chǎn/
my sister	พี่สาวของผม /ฉัน/,
	น้องสาวของผม /ฉัน/
	phêe sǎao khǒrng phǒm /chǎn/,
	nóng sǎao khǒrng phǒm /chǎn/
my son	ลูกชายของผม /ฉัน/
	lôok chaai khǒrng phǒm /chǎn/
my daughter	ลูกสาวของผม /ฉัน/
	lôok sǎao khǒrng phǒm /chǎn/

This is our son.	นี่คือลูกชายของเรา
	nêe kheu lôok chaai khǒrng rao
This is our daughter.	นี่คือลูกสาวของเรา
	nêe kheu lôok sǎao khǒrng rao
These are my children.	นี่คือลูก ๆ ของผม /ฉัน/
	nêe kheu lôok lôok khǒrng phǒm /chǎn/
These are our children.	นี่คือลูก ๆ ของเรา
	nêe kheu lôok lôok khǒrng rao

Farewells

Good bye!	ลาก่อนครับ /ค่ะ/! laa gòrn khráp /khâ/
Bye! (inform.)	บาย! baai
See you tomorrow.	พบกันพรุ่งนี้ครับ /ค่ะ/ phóp gan phrûng-née khráp /khâ/
See you soon.	พบกันใหม่ phóp gan mài
See you at seven.	เจอกันตอนเจ็ดโมง jer gan dtorn jèt mohng
Have fun!	ขอให้สนุกนะ! khǒr hâi sà-nùk ná
Talk to you later.	แล้วคุยกันทีหลังนะ láew khui gan thee lǎng ná
Have a nice weekend.	ขอให้มีความสุขมาก ๆ ในวันหยุดสุดสัปดาห์นี้นะ khǒr hâi mee khwaam sùk mâak mâak nai wan yùt sùt sàp-daa née ná
Good night.	ราตรีสวัสดิ์ครับ /ค่ะ/ raa-dtree sà-wàt khráp /khâ/
It's time for me to go.	ผม /ฉัน/ ต้องไปแล้ว phǒm /chǎn/ dtôrng bpai láew
I have to go.	ผม /ฉัน/ ต้องไปแล้ว phǒm /chǎn/ dtôrng bpai láew
I will be right back.	ผม /ฉัน/ จะกลับมาอีก phǒm /chǎn/ jà glàp maa èek
It's late.	ดึกแล้ว dèuk láew
I have to get up early.	ผม /ฉัน/ ต้องตื่นแต่เช้า phǒm /chǎn/ dtôrng dtèun dtàe cháo
I'm leaving tomorrow.	ผม /ฉัน/ จะออกจากพรุ่งนี้ phǒm /chǎn/ jà òrk jàak phrûng-née
We're leaving tomorrow.	เราจะออกจากพรุ่งนี้ rao jà òrk jàak phrûng-née
Have a nice trip!	เที่ยวให้สนุกนะ thîeow hâi sà-nùk ná
It was nice meeting you.	ดีใจที่ได้พบคุณครับ /ค่ะ/ dee jai thêe dâai phóp khun khráp /khâ/

It was nice talking to you.

ดีใจที่ได้คุย
กับคุณครับ /ค่ะ/
dee jai thêe dâai khui
gàp khun khráp /khâ/

Thanks for everything.

ขอบคุณสำหรับ
ทุกสิ่งครับ /ค่ะ/
khòrp khun sǎm-ràp
thúk sìng khráp /khâ/

I had a very good time.

ผม /ฉัน/ มีความสนุก
phǒm /chǎn/ mee khwaam sà-nùk

We had a very good time.

เรามีความสนุก
rao mee khwaam sà-nùk

It was really great.

มันยอดเยี่ยมมากจริง ๆ
man yôrt yîam mâak jing jing

I'm going to miss you.

ผม /ฉัน/ จะคิดถึงคุณ
phǒm /chǎn/ jà khít thěung khun

We're going to miss you.

เราจะคิดถึงคุณ
rao jà khít thěung khun

Good luck!

โชคดี!
chôhk dee

Say hi to …

ฝากสวัสดีให้...
fàak sà-wàt-dee hâi

Foreign language

I don't understand.	ผม /ฉัน/ ไม่เข้าใจ phǒm /chǎn/ mâi khâo jai
Write it down, please.	ขอเขียนให้ดูหน่อย khǒr khǐan hâi doo nòi
Do you speak …?	คุณพูดภาษา…ไหมครับ /คะ/ khun phôot phaa-sǎa…mǎi khráp /khá/

I speak a little bit of …	ผม /ฉัน/ พูดภาษา… ได้นิดหน่อย phǒm /chǎn/ phôot phaa-sǎa… dâai nít nòi
English	ภาษาอังกฤษ phaa-sǎa ang-grìt
Turkish	ภาษาตุรกี phaa-sǎa dtù-rá-gee
Arabic	ภาษาอารบิค phaa-sǎa aa-rá-bìk
French	ภาษาฝรั่งเศส phaa-sǎa fà-ràng-sàyt

German	ภาษาเยอรมัน phaa-sǎa yer-rá-man
Italian	ภาษาอิตาเลี่ยน phaa-sǎa i dtaa lîan
Spanish	ภาษาสเปน phaa-sǎa sà-bpayn
Portuguese	ภาษาโปรตุเกส phaa-sǎa bproh-dtù-gàyt
Chinese	ภาษาจีน phaa-sǎa jeen
Japanese	ภาษาญี่ปุ่น phaa-sǎa yêe-bpùn

Can you repeat that, please.	ขอพูดอีกครั้งหนึ้งครับ /คะ/ khǒr phôot èek khráng nêung khráp /khá/
I understand.	ผม /ฉัน/ เข้าใจ phǒm /chǎn/ khâo jai
I don't understand.	ผม /ฉัน/ ไม่เข้าใจ phǒm /chǎn/ mâi khâo jai
Please speak more slowly.	ขอพูดช้า ๆ ครับ /ค่ะ/ khǒr phôot cháa cháa khráp /khâ/

Is that correct? (Am I saying it right?) นี่ถูกต้องไหม
nêe thòok dtôrng măi

What is this? (What does this mean?) นี่คืออะไร
nêe kheu a-rai

Apologies

Excuse me, please.

ขอโทษครับ /ค่ะ/
khŏr thôht khráp /khâ/

I'm sorry.

ผม /ฉัน/ เสียใจ
phŏm /chǎn/ sĭa jai

I'm really sorry.

ผม /ฉัน/ เสียใจจริง ๆ
phŏm /chǎn/ sĭa jai jing jing

Sorry, it's my fault.

ขอโทษ นี่เป็นความผิด
ของผม /ฉัน/
khŏr thôht · nêe bpen khwaam phìt
khŏrng phŏm /chǎn/

My mistake.

นี่เป็นความผิด
ของผม /ฉัน/ เอง
nêe bpen khwaam phìt
khŏrng phŏm /chǎn/ ayng

May I ...?

ผม /ฉัน/... ได้ไหม
phŏm /chǎn/... dâai măi

Do you mind if I ...?

คุณจะรังเกียจไหม
ถ้าผม /ฉัน/ จะ...
khun jà rang gìat măi khráp
thâa phŏm /chǎn/ jà...

It's OK.

ไม่เป็นไร
mâi bpen rai

It's all right.

ไม่เป็นไร
mâi bpen rai

Don't worry about it.

ไม่ต้องเป็นห่วงครับ /ค่ะ/
mâi dtôrng bpen hùang khráp /khâ/

Agreement

Yes.	ใช่ châi
Yes, sure.	ใช่ แน่นอน châi · nâe norn
OK (Good!)	โอเค! oh khay
Very well.	ดีมาก dee mâak
Certainly!	แน่นอน! nâe norn
I agree.	ผม /ฉัน/ เห็นด้วย phǒm /chǎn/ hěn dûay
That's correct.	ถูกต้อง thòok dtôrng
That's right.	ถูกต้อง thòok dtôrng
You're right.	ถูกต้อง thòok dtôrng
I don't mind.	ผม /ฉัน/ ไม่ขัดข้อง phǒm /chǎn/ mâi khàt không
Absolutely right.	ถูกต้อง thòok dtôrng
It's possible.	เป็นไปได้ bpen bpai dâai
That's a good idea.	นี่เป็นความคิดที่ดี nêe bpen khwaam khít thêe dee
I can't say no.	ผม /ฉัน/ ปฏิเสธไม่ได้ phǒm /chǎn/ bpà-dtì-sàyt mâi dâai
I'd be happy to.	ผม /ฉัน/ จะยินดี phǒm /chǎn/ jà yin dee
With pleasure.	ด้วยความยินดี dûay khwaam yin dee

Refusal. Expressing doubt

No.
ไม่ใช่
mâi châi

Certainly not.
ไม่ใช่ แน่
mâi châi· nâe

I don't agree.
ผม /ฉัน/ ไม่เห็นด้วย
phŏm /chăn/ mâi hĕn dûay

I don't think so.
ผม /ฉัน/ ไม่คิดอย่างนี้
phŏm /chăn/ mâi khít yàang née

It's not true.
นี่ไม่เป็นความจริง
nêe mâi bpen khwaam jing

You are wrong.
คุณผิดไปแล้วครับ /ค่ะ/
khun phìt bpai láew khráp /khâ/

I think you are wrong.
ผม /ฉัน/ คิดว่าคุณผิด
phŏm /chăn/ khít wâa khun phìt

I'm not sure.
ผม /ฉัน/ ไม่แน่ใจ
phŏm /chăn/ mâi nâe jai

It's impossible.
เป็นไปไม่ได้
bpen bpai mâi dâi

Nothing of the kind (sort)!
ไม่มีทาง!
mâi mee thaang

The exact opposite.
ตรงกันข้าม
dtrong gan khâam

I'm against it.
ผม /ฉัน/ ไม่เห็นด้วย
phŏm /chăn/ mâi hĕn dûay

I don't care.
ผม /ฉัน/ ไม่สนใจ
phŏm /chăn/ mâi sŏn jai

I have no idea.
ผม /ฉัน/ ไม่รู้เลย
phŏm /chăn/ mâi róo loie

I doubt it.
ผม /ฉัน/ สงสัย
phŏm /chăn/ sŏng-săi

Sorry, I can't.
ขอโทษ ผม /ฉัน/
ไม่ได้ครับ /คะ/
khŏr thôht · phŏm /chăn/
mâi dâai khráp /khâ/

Sorry, I don't want to.
ขอโทษ ผม /ฉัน/ ,
ไม่ต้องการครับ /คะ/
khŏr thôht · phŏm /chăn/
mâi dtôrng gaan khráp /khâ/

Thank you, but I don't need this.
ขอบคุณ แต่ผม /ฉัน/
ไม่ต้องการครับ /คะ/
khòrp khun · dtàe phŏm /chăn/
mâi dtôrng gaan khráp /khâ/

It's getting late.	ดึกแล้ว
	dèuk láew
I have to get up early.	ผม /ฉัน/ ต้องตื่นแต่เช้า
	phǒm /chǎn/ dtôrng dtèun dtàe cháo
I don't feel well.	ผม /ฉัน/ รู้สึกไม่สบาย
	phǒm /chǎn/ róo sèuk mâi sà-baai

Expressing gratitude

Thank you.
ขอบคุณครับ /ค่ะ/
khòrp khun khráp /khâ/

Thank you very much.
ขอบคุณมาก
khòrp khun mâak

I really appreciate it.
รู้สึกขอบคุณจริง ๆ
róo sèuk khòrp khun jing jing

I'm really grateful to you.
ผม /ฉัน/ รู้สึกขอบคุณ
จริง ๆ ครับ /ค่ะ/
phŏm /chăn/ róo sèuk khòrp khun
jing jing khráp /khâ/

We are really grateful to you.
เรารู้สึกขอบคุณ
จริง ๆ ครับ /ค่ะ/
rao róo sèuk khòrp khun
jing jing khráp /khâ/

Thank you for your time.
ขอบคุณสำหรับเวลา
ของคุณครับ /คะ/
khòrp khun săm-ràp way-laa
khŏrng khun khráp /khâ/

Thanks for everything.
ขอบคุณสำหรับ
ทุกสิ่งครับ /คะ/
khòrp khun săm-ràp
thúk sìng khráp /khâ/

Thank you for ...
ขอบคุณสำหรับ...ครับ /ค่ะ/
khòrp khun săm-ràp…khráp /khâ/

your help
ความช่วยเหลือของคุณ
khwaam chûay lĕua khŏrng khun

a nice time
ช่วงเวลาที่ดี
chûang way-laa thêe dee

a wonderful meal
อาหารที่วิเศษ
aa hăan thêe wí-sàyt

a pleasant evening
ช่วงเวลาเย็นที่ดีเยี่ยม
chûang way-laa yen thêe dee yîam

a wonderful day
วันที่แสนวิเศษ
wan thêe săen wí-sàyt

an amazing journey
การเดินทางที่น่าสนใจ
gaan dern thaang têe nâa sŏn jai

Don't mention it.
ไม่เป็นไรครับ /ค่ะ/
mâi bpen rai khráp /khâ/

You are welcome.
ไม่เป็นไรครับ /ค่ะ/
mâi bpen rai khráp /khâ/

Any time.
ม่เป็นไรครับ /ค่ะ/
mâi bpen rai khráp /khâ/

My pleasure.

ยินดีที่ช่วยครับ /ค่ะ/
yin dee thêe chûay khráp /khâ/

Forget it.

ไม่เป็นไรครับ /ค่ะ/
mâi bpen rai khráp /khâ/

Don't worry about it.

ไม่เป็นไรครับ /ค่ะ/
mâi bpen rai khráp /khâ/

Congratulations. Best wishes

Congratulations!	ขอแสดงความยินดี! khǒr sà-daeng khwaam yin-dee
Happy birthday!	สุขสันต์วันเกิด! sùk-sǎn wan gèrt
Merry Christmas!	สุขสันต์วันคริสต์มาส! sùk-sǎn wan khrít-mâat
Happy New Year!	สวัสดีปีใหม่! sà-wàt-dee bpee mài

Happy Easter!	สุขสันต์วันอีสเตอร์! sùk-sǎn wan èet-dtêr
Happy Hanukkah!	สุขสันต์วันฮานุกกะห์! sùk-sǎn wan haa núk-gà

I'd like to propose a toast.	ผม /ฉัน/ อยากจะขอดื่มอวยพร phǒm /chǎn/ yàak jà khǒr dèum uay phon
Cheers!	ไชโย! chai-yoh
Let's drink to …!	ขอดื่มให้…! khǒr dèum hâi…
To our success!	ความสำเร็จของเรา! khwaam sǎm-rèt khǒrng rao
To your success!	ความสำเร็จของคุณ! khwaam sǎm-rèt khǒrng khun

Good luck!	โชคดี! chôhk dee
Have a nice day!	ขอให้วันนี้เป็นวันที่ดี ครับ /คะ/! khǒr hâi wan née bpen wan thêe dee khráp /khâ/
Have a good holiday!	ขอให้วันหยุดมีความสุข ครับ /คะ/! khǒr hâi wan yùt mee khwaam sùk khráp /khâ/
Have a safe journey!	ขอให้เดินทางปลอดภัย ครับ /คะ/! khǒr hâi dern thaang bplòrt phai khráp /khâ/
I hope you get better soon!	ขอให้คุณหายโดยเร็วครับ /ค่ะ/! khǒr hâi khun hǎai doi reo khráp /khâ/

Socializing

Why are you sad?	คุณเศร้าทำไม khun sâo tham-mai
Smile! Cheer up!	ยิ้มเข้าไว้! yím khâo wái
Are you free tonight?	คืนนี้คุณว่างไหม kheun née khun wâang măi

May I offer you a drink?	ขอผม /ฉัน/ เลี้ยงเครื่องดื่มให้คุณ khŏr phŏm /chăn/ líang khrêuang dèum hâi khun
Would you like to dance?	คุณอยากเต้นรำไหมครับ khun yàak dtên ram măi
Let's go to the movies.	ไปดูหนังกันเถอะ bpai doo năng gan thùh

May I invite you to …?	ขอเชิญคุณไป khŏr chern khun bpai
a restaurant	ร้านอาหาร ráan aa-hăan
the movies	โรงภาพยนต์ rohng phâa-pha-yon
the theater	โรงละคร rohng lá-khon
go for a walk	ไปเดินเล่น bpai dern lên

At what time?	กี่โมง gèe mohng
tonight	คืนนี้ kheun née
at six	หกโมง hòk mohng
at seven	เจ็ดโมง jèt mohng
at eight	แปดโมง bpàet mohng
at nine	เก้าโมง gâo mohng

Do you like it here?	คุณชอบที่นี่ไหม khun chôrp thêe nêe măi
Are you here with someone?	คุณมาที่นี่กับใครหรือเปล่า khun maa thêe nêe gàp khrai rĕu bplào

I'm with my friend.

ผม /ฉัน/ มากับเพื่อน
ของผม /ฉัน/
phǒm /chǎn/ maa gàp phêuan
khǒrng phǒm /chǎn/

I'm with my friends.

ผม /ฉัน/ มากับเพื่อน ๆ
ของผม /ฉัน/
phǒm /chǎn/ maa gàp phêuan phêuan
khǒrng phǒm /chǎn/

No, I'm alone.

ผม /ฉัน/ มาเป็นคนเดียว
phǒm /chǎn/ maa bpen khon dieow

Do you have a boyfriend?

คุณมีแฟนไหม
khun mee faen mǎi

I have a boyfriend.

ฉันมีแฟนแล้ว
chǎn mee faen láew

Do you have a girlfriend?

คุณมีแฟนไหม
khun mee faen mǎi

I have a girlfriend.

ผมมีแฟนแล้ว
phǒm mee faen láew

Can I see you again?

ผม /ฉัน/ เจอคุณอีกได้ไหม
phǒm /chǎn/ jer khun èek dâai mǎi

Can I call you?

ผม /ฉัน/ โทรหาคุณได้ไหม
phǒm /chǎn/ thoh hǎa khun dâai mǎi

Call me. (Give me a call.)

แล้วโทรมานะ
láew thoh maa ná

What's your number?

เบอร์คุณคืออะไร
ber khun kheu a-rai

I miss you.

ผม /ฉัน/ คิดถึงคุณ
phǒm /chǎn/ khít thěung khun

You have a beautiful name.

ชื่อคุณเพราะครับ
chêu kun phrór khráp

I love you.

ผม /ฉัน/ รักคุณ
phǒm /chǎn/ rák khun

Will you marry me?

คุณจะแต่งงานกับ
ผม /ฉัน/ ไหม
khun jà dtàeng ngaan gàp
phǒm /chǎn/ mǎi

You're kidding!

คุณล้อเล่น!
khun lór lên

I'm just kidding.

ผม /ฉัน/ แค่ล้อเล่น
phǒm /chǎn/ khâe lór lên

Are you serious?

คุณจริงจังไหมครับ /คะ/
khun jing jang mǎi khráp /khá/

I'm serious.

ผม /ฉัน/ จริงจัง
phǒm /chǎn/ jing jang

Really?!

จริงเหรอ!
jing rěr

It's unbelievable!

ไม่น่าเชื่อ!
mâi nâa chêua

I don't believe you.	ผม /ฉัน/ ไม่เชื่อคุณ
	phŏm /chăn/ mâi chêua khun
I can't.	ผม /ฉัน/ ทำไม่ได้
	phŏm /chăn/ tham mâi dâai
I don't know.	ผม /ฉัน/ ไม่รู้
	phŏm /chăn/ mâi róo
I don't understand you.	ผม /ฉัน/ไม่เข้าใจคุณ
	phŏm /chăn/ mâi khâo jai khun
Please go away.	กรุณาไปเถอะ
	gà-rú-naa bpai thùh
Leave me alone!	ผม /ฉัน/ ขออยู่คนเดียว
	phŏm /chăn/ khŏr yòo khon dieow

I can't stand him.	ผม /ฉัน/ ทนเขาไม่ได้
	phŏm /chăn/ ton khăo mâi dâai
You are disgusting!	คุณน่ารังเกียจ!
	khun nâa rang gìat
I'll call the police!	ผม /ฉัน/ จะโทรเรียกตำรวจ!
	phŏm /chăn/ jà thoh rîak dtam-rùat

Sharing impressions. Emotions

I like it.	ผม /ฉัน/ ชอบมันนะ phǒm /chǎn/ chôrp man ná
Very nice.	ดีมาก dee mâak
That's great!	ยอดเยี่ยม! yôrt yîam
It's not bad.	ไม่เลว mâi leo
I don't like it.	ผม /ฉัน/ ไม่ชอบมัน phǒm /chǎn/ mâi chôrp man
It's not good.	ไม่ดี mâi dee
It's bad.	แย่ yâe
It's very bad.	แย่มาก yâe mâak
It's disgusting.	น่ารังเกียจ nâa rang gìat
I'm happy.	ผม /ฉัน/ มีความสุข phǒm /chǎn/ mee khwaam sùk
I'm content.	ผม /ฉัน/ พอใจ phǒm /chǎn/ phor jai
I'm in love.	ผม /ฉัน/ มีความรัก phǒm /chǎn/ mee khwaam rák
I'm calm.	ผม /ฉัน/ สงบ phǒm /chǎn/ sà-ngòp
I'm bored.	ผม /ฉัน/ เบื่อ phǒm /chǎn/ bèua
I'm tired.	ผม /ฉัน/ เหนื่อย phǒm nèuay /chǎn nèuay/
I'm sad.	ผม /ฉัน/ เศร้า phǒm /chǎn/ sâo
I'm frightened.	ผม /ฉัน/ กลัว phǒm /chǎn/ glua
I'm angry.	ผม /ฉัน/ โกรธ phǒm /chǎn/ gròht
I'm worried.	ผม /ฉัน/ กังวล phǒm /chǎn/ gang-won
I'm nervous.	ผม /ฉัน/ ประหม่า phǒm /chǎn/ bprà-màa

I'm jealous. (envious)

ผม /ฉัน/ อิจฉา
phǒm /chǎn/ ìt-chǎa

I'm surprised.

ผม /ฉัน/ แปลกใจ
phǒm /chǎn/ bplàek jai

I'm perplexed.

ผม /ฉัน/ งงงวย
phǒm /chǎn/ ngong-nguay

Problems. Accidents

I've got a problem.	ผม /ฉัน/ มีปัญหา
	phŏm /chăn/ mee bpan-hăa
We've got a problem.	เรามีปัญหา
	rao mee bpan-hăa
I'm lost.	ผม /ฉัน/ หลงทาง
	phŏm /chăn/ lŏng thaang
I missed the last bus (train).	ผม /ฉัน/ ขาดรถเมล์ (รถไฟ) สุดทาย
	phŏm /chăn/ khàat rót mae (rót fai) sùt tháai
I don't have any money left.	ผม /ฉัน/ ไม่มีเงินเหลือเลย
	phŏm /chăn/ mâi mee ngern lĕua loie
I've lost my …	ผม /ฉัน/ ทำ...ของผม /ฉัน/ หาย
	phŏm /chăn/ tham...khŏrng phŏm /chăn/ hăai
Someone stole my …	มีใครขโมย...ของผม /ฉัน/ ไป
	mee khrai khà-moi...khŏrng phŏm /chăn/ bpai
passport	หนังสือเดินทาง
	năng-sĕu dern-thaang
wallet	กระเป๋าเงิน
	grà-bpăo ngern
papers	เอกสาร
	àyk-ka -săan
ticket	ตั๋ว
	dtŭa
money	เงิน
	ngern
handbag	กระเป๋าถือ
	grà-bpăo thĕu
camera	กล้องถ่ายรูป
	glôrng thàai rôop
laptop	แล็ปท็อป
	láep-thóp
tablet computer	คอมพิวเตอร์แท็บเล็ต
	khorm-phiw-dtêr tháep lét
mobile phone	มือถือ
	meu thĕu

Help me!   ช่วยด้วยครับ /ค่ะ/!
chûay dûay khráp /khâ/

What's happened?   เกิดอะไรขึ้น
gèrt a-rai khêun

fire   ไฟไหม้
fai mâi

shooting   การยิง
gaan ying

murder   ฆาตกรรม
khâat-dtà-gaam

explosion   การระเบิด
gaan rá-bèrt

fight   การต่อสู้
gaan dtòr sôo

Call the police!   ขอโทรเรียกตำรวจ!
khŏr thoh rîak dtam-rùat

Please hurry up!   เร็ว ๆ หน่อยครับ /ค่ะ/!
reo reo nòi khráp /khâ/

I'm looking for the police station.   ผม /ฉัน/ กำลังหา สถานีตำรวจ
phŏm /chăn/ gam-lang hăa sà-thăa-nee dtam-rùat

I need to make a call.   ผม /ฉัน/ ต้องการโทร
phŏm /chăn/ dtôrng gaan thoh

May I use your phone?   ผม /ฉัน/ ใช้โทรศัพท์ ของคุณได้ไหม
phŏm /chăn/ chái thoh-rá-sàp khŏrng khun dâai măi

I've been ...   ผม /ฉัน/ ถูก...
phŏm /chăn/ thòok...

mugged   ชิงทรัพย์
ching sáp

robbed   ปล้น
bplôn

raped   ข่มขืน
khòm khĕun

attacked (beaten up)   ซ้อม
sóm

Are you all right?   คุณเป็นอย่างไรบ้างครับ /คะ/
khun bpen yàang rai bâang khráp /khá/

Did you see who it was?   คุณเห็นไหมครับ /คะ/ ว่าเป็นใคร
khun hĕn măi khráp /khá/ wâa bpen khrai

Would you be able to recognize the person?   คุณจำหน้าคนร้ายได้ไหม
khun jam nâa khon ráai dâai măi

Are you sure?   คุณแน่ใจไหม
khun nâe jai măi

Please calm down.   กรุณาใจเย็น ๆ ครับ /ค่ะ/
gà-rú-naa jai yen khráp /khâ/

Take it easy!

ใจเย็น
jai yen

Don't worry!

ไม่ต้องเป็นห่วง!
mâi dtôrng bpen hùang

Everything will be fine.

ทุกอย่างจะดีขึ้นเอง
thúk yàang jà dee khêun ayng

Everything's all right.

ทุกอย่างเรียบร้อย
thúk yàang rîap rói

Come here, please.

ขอมาที่นี่หน่อยครับ /ค่ะ/
khŏr maa thêe nêe nòi khráp /khâ/

I have some questions for you.

ผม /ฉัน/ มีบางคำถาม
phŏm /chăn/ mee baang kham thăam

Wait a moment, please.

กรุณารอสักครู่ครับ /ค่ะ/
gà-rú-naa ror sàk khrôo khráp /khâ/

Do you have any I.D.?

คุณมีบัตรประจำตัวอะไรไหม
ครับ /ค่ะ/
khun mee bàt bprà-jam dtua a-rai măi
khráp /khá/

Thanks. You can leave now.

ขอบคุณ คุณไปได้แล้ว
khòrp khun · khun bpai dâai láew

Hands behind your head!

มือขึ้น
meu khêun

You're under arrest!

คุณถูกจับแล้ว
khun thòok jàp láew

Health problems

Please help me.	กรุณาช่วยผม /ฉัน/ gà-rú-naa chûay phŏm /chăn/
I don't feel well.	ผม /ฉัน/ รู้สึกไม่สบาย phŏm /chăn/ róo sèuk mâi sà-baai
My husband doesn't feel well.	สามีของฉันไม่สบาย săa-mee khŏrng chăn mâi sà-baai
My son ...	ลูกชายของผม /ฉัน/... lôok chaai khŏrng phŏm /chăn/...
My father ...	พ่อของผม /ฉัน/... phôr khŏrng phŏm /chăn/...
My wife doesn't feel well.	ภรรยาของผมไม่สบาย phan-rá-yaa khŏrng phŏm mâi sà-baai
My daughter ...	ลูกสาวของผม /ฉัน/... lôok săao khŏrng phŏm /chăn/...
My mother ...	แม่ของผม /ฉัน/... mâe khŏrng phŏm /chăn/...
I've got a ...	ผม /ฉัน/... phŏm /chăn/...
headache	ปวดหัว bpùat hŭa
sore throat	เจ็บคอ jèp khor
stomach ache	ปวดท้อง bpùat thórng
toothache	ปวดฟัน bpùat fan
I feel dizzy.	ผม /ฉัน/ รู้สึกเวียนหัว phŏm /chăn/ róo sèuk wian hŭa
He has a fever.	เขามีไข้ khăo mee khâi
She has a fever.	เธอมีไข้ ther mee khâi
I can't breathe.	ผม /ฉัน/ หายใจไม่ออก phŏm /chăn/ hăai-jai mâi òrk
I'm short of breath.	ผม /ฉัน/ หายใจไม่ออก phŏm /chăn/ hăai-jai mâi òrk
I am asthmatic.	ผม /ฉัน/ มีโรคหืด phŏm /chăn/ mee rôhk hèut
I am diabetic.	ผม /ฉัน/ มีโรคเบาหวาน phŏm /chăn/ mee rôhk bao wăan

I can't sleep.

ผม /ฉัน/ นอนไม่หลับ
phŏm /chăn/ norn mâi làp

food poisoning

กินอาหารเป็นพิษ
gin aa hăan bpen phít

It hurts here.

เจ็บที่นี่
jèp thêe nêe

Help me!

ขอช่วยครับ /ค่ะ/!
khŏr chûay khráp /khâ/

I am here!

ผม /ฉัน/ อยู่ที่นี่
phŏm /chăn/ yòo thêe nêe

We are here!

เราอยู่ที่นี่
rao yòo thêe nêe

Get me out of here!

ขอเอาผม /ฉัน/
ออกไปจากที่นี่
khŏr ao phŏm /chăn/
òk bpai jàak thêe nêe

I need a doctor.

ผม /ฉัน/ ต้องไปหาหมอ
phŏm /chăn/ dtông bpai hăa mŏr

I can't move.

ผม /ฉัน/ ขยับไม่ได้
phŏm /chăn/ khà-yàp mâi dâai

I can't move my legs.

ผม /ฉัน/ ขยับขาของผม
/ฉัน/ ไม่ได้
phŏm /chăn/ khà-yàp khăa khŏrng phŏm
/chăn/ mâi dâai

I have a wound.

ผม /ฉัน/ มีแผล
phŏm /chăn/ mee phlăe

Is it serious?

อาการหนักไหม
aa-gaan nàk măi

My documents are in my pocket.

เอกสารของผม /ฉัน/
อยู่ในกระเป๋าของผม /ฉัน/
àyk săan khŏrng phŏm /chăn/
yòo nai grà-bpăo khŏrng phŏm /chăn/

Calm down!

ใจเย็น
jai yen

May I use your phone?

ผม /ฉัน/ ใช้โทรศัพท์
ของคุณได้ไหม
phŏm /chăn/ chái thoh-rá-sàp
khŏrng khun dâai măi

Call an ambulance!

ขอโทรเรียกรถพยาบาล!
khŏr thoh rîak rót phá-yaa-baan

It's urgent!

เรื่องด่วน!
rêuang dùan

It's an emergency!

เรื่องฉุกเฉิน
rêuang chùk-chĕrn

Please hurry up!

กรุณารีบด้วยครับ /ค่ะ/!
gà-rú-naa rêep dûay khráp /khâ/

Would you please call a doctor?

ขอโทรเรียกหมอครับ /ค่ะ/
khŏr thoh rîak mŏr khráp /khá/

Where is the hospital?

โรงพยาบาลอยู่ที่ไหน
rohng phá-yaa-baan yòo thêe năi

How are you feeling?	คุณรู้สึกอย่างไรบ้าง ครับ /คะ/ khun róo sèuk yàang rai bâang khráp /khá/
Are you all right?	คุณรู้สึกสบายดีไหม khun róo sèuk sà-baai dee măi
What's happened?	เกิดอะไรขึ้น gèrt a-rai khêun
I feel better now.	ผม /ฉัน/ ดีขึ้นแล้ว phŏm /chăn/ dee khêun láew
It's OK.	ผม /ฉัน/ สบายดี phŏm /chăn/ sà-baai dee
It's all right.	ไม่เป็นไร mâi bpen rai

At the pharmacy

pharmacy (drugstore)	ร้านขายยา ráan khǎai yaa
24-hour pharmacy	ร้านขายยา 24 ชั่วโมง ráan khǎai yaa · yêe sìp sèe · chûa mohng
Where is the closest pharmacy?	ร้านขายยาที่ใกล้ ที่สุดอยู่ที่ไหน ráan khǎai yaa thêe glâi thêe sùt yòo thêe nǎi
Is it open now?	ตอนนี้มันเปิดไหม dtorn-née man bpèrt mǎi
At what time does it open?	มันเปิดกี่โมง man bpèrt gèe mohng
At what time does it close?	มันปิดกี่โมง man bpìt gèe mohng
Is it far?	อยู่ไกลไหม yòo glai mǎi
Can I get there on foot?	ผม /ฉัน/ เดินไปที่นั่นได้ไหม phǒm /chǎn/ dern bpai thêe nân dâai mǎi
Can you show me on the map?	ขอชี้ให้ผม /ฉัน/ ดูในแผนที่ครับ /คะ/ khǒr chée hâi phǒm /chǎn/ doo nai phǎen thêe khráp /khá/
Please give me something for ...	ช่วยหาอะไรสำหรับอาการ... chûay hǎa a-rai sǎm-ràp aa-gaan...
a headache	ปวดหัว bpùat hǔa
a cough	ไอ ai
a cold	เป็นหวัด bpen wàt
the flu	ไข้หวัด khâi wàt
a fever	เป็นไข้ bpen khâi
a stomach ache	ปวดท้อง bpùat thórng
nausea	คลื่นไส้ khlêun sâi

| diarrhea | ท้องเสีย
thórng sǐa |
| constipation | ท้องผูก
thórng phòok |

pain in the back	ปวดหลัง bpùat lǎng
chest pain	ปวดหน้าอก bpùat nâa òk
side stitch	ปวดข้าง bpùat khâang
abdominal pain	ปวดท้อง bpùat thórng

pill	ยาเม็ด yaa mét
ointment, cream	ครีม khreem
syrup	น้ำเชื่อม náam chêuam
spray	สเปรย์ sà-bpray
drops	ยาหยอด yaa yòrt

You need to go to the hospital.	คุณต้องไปโรงพยาบาล khun dtôrng bpai rohng phá-yaa-baan
health insurance	ใบประกันสุขภาพ bai bprà-gan sùk-khà-pâap
prescription	ใบสั่งยา bai sàng yaa
insect repellant	ยากำจัดแมลง yaa gam-jàt má-laeng
Band Aid	ปลาสเตอร์ pláat-dtêr

The bare minimum

Excuse me, …	ขอโทษครับ /ค่ะ/ khŏr thôht khráp /khâ/
Hello.	สวัสดีครับ /สวัสดีค่ะ/ sà-wàt-dee khráp /sà-wàt-dee khâ/
Thank you.	ขอบคุณครับ /ค่ะ/ khòrp khun khráp /khâ/
Good bye.	สวัสดีครับ /สวัสดีค่ะ/ sà-wàt-dee khráp /sà-wàt-dee khâ/
Yes.	ใช่ châi
No.	ไม่ใช่ mâi châi
I don't know.	ผม /ฉัน/ ไม่ทราบ phŏm /chăn/ mâi-sâap
Where? | Where to? | When?	ที่ไหน | ไปที่ไหน | เมื่อไหร่ thêe năi | bpai thêe năi | mêua rài
I need …	ผม /ฉัน/ ต้องการ... phŏm /chăn/ dtôrng gaan…
I want …	ผม /ฉัน/ ต้องการ... phŏm /chăn/ dtôrng gaan…
Do you have ...?	คุณมี...ไหมครับ /คะ/ khun mee…măi khráp /khá/
Is there a … here?	ที่นี่มี...ไหม thêe nêe mee…măi
May I ...?	ผม /ฉัน/ ขออนุญาต... phŏm /chăn/ khŏr a-nú-yâat…
…, please (polite request)	โปรด... bpròht…
I'm looking for …	ผม /ฉัน/ กำลังหา... phŏm /chăn/ gam-lang hăa…
the restroom	ห้องน้ำ hôrng náam
an ATM	เอทีเอ็ม ay thee em
a pharmacy (drugstore)	ร้านขายยา ráan khăai yaa
a hospital	โรงพยาบาล rohng phá-yaa-baan
the police station	สถานีตำรวจ sà-thăa-nee dtam-rùat
the subway	รถไฟใต้ดิน rót fai dtâi din

a taxi	รถแท็กซี่
	rót tháek-sêe
the train station	สถานีรถไฟ
	sà-thǎa-nee rót fai

My name is ...	ผม /ฉัน/ ชื่อ...
	phǒm /chǎn/ chêu…
What's your name?	คุณชื่ออะไรครับ /คะ/
	khun chêu a-rai khráp /khá/
Could you please help me?	ขอช่วยผมหน่อยครับ
	/ขอช่วยฉันหน่อยคะ/
	khǒr chûay phǒm nòi khráp
	/khǒr chûay chǎn nòi khá/
I've got a problem.	ผม /ฉัน/ มีปัญหา
	phǒm /chǎn/ mee bpan-hǎa
I don't feel well.	ผม /ฉัน/ รู้สึกไม่สบาย
	phǒm /chǎn/ róo sèuk mâi sà-baai
Call an ambulance!	ขอเรียกรถพยาบาล!
	khǒr rîak rót phá-yaa-baan
May I make a call?	ผม /ฉัน/ โทรศัพท์ได้ไหม
	phǒm /chǎn/ thoh-rá-sàp dâai mǎi

I'm sorry.	ขอโทษ
	khǒr thôht
You're welcome.	ไม่เป็นไรครับ /ค่ะ/
	mâi bpen rai khráp /khâ/

I, me	ผม /ฉัน/
	phǒm /chǎn/
you (inform.)	คุณ
	khun
he	เขา
	khǎo
she	เธอ
	ther
they (masc.)	พวกเขา
	phûak khǎo
they (fem.)	พวกเขา
	phûak khǎo
we	เรา
	rao
you (pl)	คุณทั้งหลาย
	khun tháng lǎai
you (sg, form.)	ท่าน
	thân

ENTRANCE	ทางเข้า
	thaang khâo
EXIT	ทางออก
	thaang òrk
OUT OF ORDER	เสีย
	sǐa

CLOSED	ปิด
	bpìt
OPEN	เปิด
	bpèrt
FOR WOMEN	สำหรับผู้หญิง
	săm-ràp phôo yǐng
FOR MEN	สำหรับผู้ชาย
	săm-ràp phôo chaai

CONCISE DICTIONARY

This section contains more than 1,500 useful words arranged alphabetically. The dictionary includes a lot of gastronomic terms and will be helpful when ordering food at a restaurant or buying groceries

T&P Books Publishing

DICTIONARY CONTENTS

T&P Books Publishing

time	เวลา	way-laa
hour	ชั่วโมง	chûa mohng
half an hour	ครึ่งชั่วโมง	khrêung chûa mohng
minute	นาที	naa-thee
second	วินาที	wí-naa-thee

today (adv)	วันนี้	wan née
tomorrow (adv)	พรุ่งนี้	phrûng-née
yesterday (adv)	เมื่อวานนี้	mêua waan née

Monday	วันจันทร์	wan jan
Tuesday	วันอังคาร	wan ang-khaan
Wednesday	วันพุธ	wan phút
Thursday	วันพฤหัสบดี	wan phá-réu-hàt-sà-bor-dee

Friday	วันศุกร์	wan sùk
Saturday	วันเสาร์	wan săo
Sunday	วันอาทิตย์	wan aa-thít

day	วัน	wan
working day	วันทำงาน	wan tham ngaan
public holiday	วันนักขัตฤกษ์	wan nák-khàt-rêrk
weekend	วันสุดสัปดาห์	wan sùt sàp-daa

week	สัปดาห์	sàp-daa
last week (adv)	สัปดาห์ก่อน	sàp-daa gòrn
next week (adv)	สัปดาห์หน้า	sàp-daa nâa

| sunrise | พระอาทิตย์ขึ้น | phrá aa-thít khêun |
| sunset | พระอาทิตย์ตก | phrá aa-thít dtòk |

| in the morning | ตอนเช้า | dtorn cháo |
| in the afternoon | ตอนบ่าย | dtorn bàai |

| in the evening | ตอนเย็น | dtorn yen |
| tonight (this evening) | คืนนี้ | kheun née |

| at night | กลางคืน | glaang kheun |
| midnight | เที่ยงคืน | thîang kheun |

January	มกราคม	mók-gà-raa khom
February	กุมภาพันธ์	gum-phaa phan
March	มีนาคม	mee-naa khom
April	เมษายน	may-săa-yon
May	พฤษภาคม	phréut-sà-phaa khom

June	มิถุนายน	mí-thù-naa-yon
July	กรกฎาคม	gà-rá-gà-daa-khom
August	สิงหาคม	sǐng hǎa khom
September	กันยายน	gan-yaa-yon
October	ตุลาคม	dtù-laa khom
November	พฤศจิกายน	phréut-sà-jì-gaa-yon
December	ธันวาคม	than-waa khom
in spring	ฤดูใบไม้ผลิ	réu-doo bai máai phlì
in summer	ฤดูร้อน	réu-doo rórn
in fall	ฤดูใบไม้ร่วง	réu-doo bai máai rûang
in winter	ฤดูหนาว	réu-doo nǎao
month	เดือน	deuan
season (summer, etc.)	ฤดูกาล	réu-doo gaan
year	ปี	bpee
century	ศตวรรษ	sà-dtà-wát

2. Numbers. Numerals

digit, figure	ตัวเลข	dtua lâyk
number	เลข	lâyk
minus sign	เครื่องหมายลบ	khrêuang mǎai lóp
plus sign	เครื่องหมายบวก	khrêuang mǎai bùak
sum, total	ผลรวม	phǒn ruam
first (adj)	แรก	râek
second (adj)	ที่สอง	thêe sǒrng
third (adj)	ที่สาม	thêe sǎam
0 zero	ศูนย์	sǒon
1 one	หนึ่ง	nèung
2 two	สอง	sǒrng
3 three	สาม	sǎam
4 four	สี่	sèe
5 five	ห้า	hâa
6 six	หก	hòk
7 seven	เจ็ด	jèt
8 eight	แปด	bpàet
9 nine	เก้า	gâo
10 ten	สิบ	sìp
11 eleven	สิบเอ็ด	sìp èt
12 twelve	สิบสอง	sìp sǒrng
13 thirteen	สิบสาม	sìp sǎam
14 fourteen	สิบสี่	sìp sèe
15 fifteen	สิบห้า	sìp hâa
16 sixteen	สิบหก	sìp hòk
17 seventeen	สิบเจ็ด	sìp jèt

| 18 eighteen | สิบแปด | sìp bpàet |
| 19 nineteen | สิบเก้า | sìp gâo |

20 twenty	ยี่สิบ	yêe sìp
30 thirty	สามสิบ	sǎam sìp
40 forty	สี่สิบ	sèe sìp
50 fifty	ห้าสิบ	hâa sìp

60 sixty	หกสิบ	hòk sìp
70 seventy	เจ็ดสิบ	jèt sìp
80 eighty	แปดสิบ	bpàet sìp
90 ninety	เก้าสิบ	gâo sìp

100 one hundred	หนึ่งร้อย	nèung rói
200 two hundred	สองร้อย	sǒrng rói
300 three hundred	สามร้อย	sǎam rói
400 four hundred	สี่ร้อย	sèe rói
500 five hundred	ห้าร้อย	hâa rói

600 six hundred	หกร้อย	hòk rói
700 seven hundred	เจ็ดร้อย	jèt rói
800 eight hundred	แปดร้อย	bpàet rói
900 nine hundred	เก้าร้อย	gâo rói
1000 one thousand	หนึ่งพัน	nèung phan

| 10000 ten thousand | หนึ่งหมื่น | nèung mèun |
| one hundred thousand | หนึ่งแสน | nèung sǎen |

| million | ล้าน | láan |
| billion | พันล้าน | phan láan |

3. Humans. Family

man (adult male)	ผู้ชาย	phôo chaai
young man	ชายหนุ่ม	chaai nùm
teenager	วัยรุ่น	wai rûn
woman	ผู้หญิง	phôo yǐng
girl (young woman)	หญิงสาว	yǐng sǎao

age	อายุ	aa-yú
adult (adj)	ผู้ใหญ่	phôo yài
middle-aged (adj)	วัยกลาง	wai glaang
elderly (adj)	วัยชรา	wai chá-raa
old (adj)	แก่	gàe

old man	ชายชรา	chaai chá-raa
old woman	หญิงชรา	yǐng chá-raa
retirement	การเกษียณอายุ	gaan gà-sǐan aa-yú
to retire (from job)	เกษียณ	gà-sǐan
retiree	ผู้เกษียณอายุ	phôo gà-sǐan aa-yú

mother	มารดา	maan-daa
father	บิดา	bì-daa
son	ลูกชาย	lôok chaai
daughter	ลูกสาว	lôok săao
elder brother	พี่ชาย	phêe chaai
younger brother	น้องชาย	nórng chaai
elder sister	พี่สาว	phêe săao
younger sister	น้องสาว	nórng săao
parents	พ่อแม่	phôr mâe
child	เด็ก, ลูก	dèk, lôok
children	เด็กๆ	dèk dèk
stepmother	แม่เลี้ยง	mâe líang
stepfather	พ่อเลี้ยง	phôr líang
grandmother	ย่า, ยาย	yâa, yaai
grandfather	ปู่, ตา	bpòo, dtaa
grandson	หลานชาย	lăan chaai
granddaughter	หลานสาว	lăan săao
grandchildren	หลานๆ	lăan
uncle	ลุง	lung
aunt	ป้า	bpâa
nephew	หลานชาย	lăan chaai
niece	หลานสาว	lăan săao
wife	ภรรยา	phan-rá-yaa
husband	สามี	săa-mee
married (masc.)	แต่งงานแล้ว	dtàeng ngaan láew
married (fem.)	แต่งงูนแล้ว	dtàeng ngaan láew
widow	แม่หม้าย	mâe mâai
widower	พ่อหม้าย	phôr mâai
name (first name)	ชื่อ	chêu
surname (last name)	นามสกุล	naam sà-gun
relative	ญาติ	yâat
friend (masc.)	เพื่อน	phêuan
friendship	มิตรภาพ	mít-dtrà-phâap
partner	หุ้นส่วน	hûn sùan
superior (n)	ผู้บังคับบัญชา	phôo bang-kháp ban-chaa
colleague	เพื่อนร่วมงาน	phêuan rûam ngaan
neighbors	เพื่อนบ้าน	phêuan bâan

4. Human body

organism (body)	ร่างกาย	râang gaai
body	ร่างกาย	râang gaai
heart	หัวใจ	hŭa jai

blood	เลือด	lêuat
brain	สมอง	sà-mŏrng
nerve	เส้นประสาท	sên bprà-sàat

bone	กระดูก	grà-dòok
skeleton	โครงกระดูก	khrohng grà-dòok
spine (backbone)	สันหลัง	săn lăng
rib	ซี่โครง	sêe khrohng
skull	กะโหลก	gà-lòhk

muscle	กล้ามเนื้อ	glâam néua
lungs	ปอด	bpòrt
skin	ผิวหนัง	phĭw năng

head	หัว	hŭa
face	หน้า	nâa
nose	จมูก	jà-mòok
forehead	หน้าผาก	nâa phàak
cheek	แก้ม	gâem

mouth	ปาก	bpàak
tongue	ลิ้น	lín
tooth	ฟัน	fan
lips	ริมฝีปาก	rim fĕe bpàak
chin	คาง	khaang

ear	หู	hŏo
neck	คอ	khor
throat	ลำคอ	lam khor

eye	ตา	dtaa
pupil	รูม่านตา	roo mâan dtaa
eyebrow	คิ้ว	khíw
eyelash	ขนตา	khŏn dtaa

hair	ผม	phŏm
hairstyle	ทรงผม	song phŏm
mustache	หนวด	nùat
beard	เครา	krao
to have (a beard, etc.)	ลงไว้	lorng wái
bald (adj)	หัวล้าน	hŭa láan

hand	มือ	meu
arm	แขน	khăen
finger	นิ้ว	níw
nail	เล็บ	lép
palm	ฝ่ามือ	fàa meu

shoulder	ไหล่	lài
leg	ขา	khăa
foot	เท้า	tháo
knee	หัวเข่า	hŭa khào

heel	ส้นเท้า	sôn tháo
back	หลัง	lăng
waist	เอว	eo
beauty mark	ไฝเสน่ห์	făi sà-này
birthmark (café au lait spot)	ปาน	bpaan

5. Medicine. Diseases. Drugs

health	สุขภาพ	sùk-khà-phâap
well (not sick)	สบายดี	sà-baai dee
sickness	โรค	rôhk
to be sick	ป่วย	bpùay
ill, sick (adj)	เจ็บป่วย	jèp bpùay

cold (illness)	หวัด	wàt
to catch a cold	เป็นหวัด	bpen wàt
tonsillitis	ตอมทอนซิลอักเสบ	dtòm thorn-sin àk-sàyp
pneumonia	โรคปอดบวม	rôhk bpòrt-buam
flu, influenza	ไขหวัดใหญ	khâi wàt yài

runny nose (coryza)	น้ำมูกไหล	nám môok lăi
cough	การไอ	gaan ai
to cough (vi)	ไอ	ai
to sneeze (vi)	จาม	jaam

stroke	โรคหลอดเลือดสมอง	rôhk lòrt lêuat sà-mŏrng
heart attack	อาการหัวใจวาย	aa-gaan hŭa jai waai
allergy	ภูมิแพ	phoom pháe
asthma	โรคหืด	rôhk hèut
diabetes	โรคเบาหวาน	rôhk bao wăan

tumor	เนื้องอก	néua ngôk
cancer	มะเร็ง	má-reng
alcoholism	โรคพิษสุราเรื้อรัง	rôhk phít sù-raa réua rang
AIDS	โรคเอดส	rôhk àyt
fever	ไข	khâi
seasickness	ภาวะเมาคลื่น	phaa-wá mao khlêun

bruise (hématome)	ฟกช้ำ	fók chám
bump (lump)	บวม	buam
to limp (vi)	กะโผลกกะเผลก	gà-phlòhk-gà-phlàyk
dislocation	ขอหลุด	khôr lùt
to dislocate (vt)	ทำขอหลุด	tham khôr lùt

fracture	กระดูกหัก	grà-dòok hàk
burn (injury)	แผลไฟไหม	phlăe fai mâi
injury	การบาดเจ็บ	gaan bàat jèp
pain, ache	ความเจ็บปวด	khwaam jèp bpùat
toothache	อาการปวดฟัน	aa-gaan bpùat fan

to sweat (perspire)	เหงื่อออก	ngèua òrk
deaf (adj)	หูหนวก	hǒo nùak
mute (adj)	เป็นใบ	bpen bâi
immunity	ภูมิคุ้มกัน	phoom khúm gan
virus	เชื้อไวรัส	chéua wai-rát
microbe	จุลินทรีย์	jù-lin-see
bacterium	แบคทีเรีย	bàek-tee-ria
infection	การติดเชื้อ	gaan dtìt chéua
hospital	โรงพยาบาล	rohng phá-yaa-baan
cure	การรักษา	gaan rák-sǎa
to vaccinate (vt)	ฉีดวัคซีน	chèet wák-seen
to be in a coma	อยู่ในอาการโคม่า	yòo nai aa-gaan khoh-mâa
intensive care	หน่วยอภิบาล	nùay à-phí-baan
symptom	อาการ	aa-gaan
pulse (heartbeat)	ชีพจร	chêep-phá-jon

6. Feelings. Emotions. Conversation

you	คุณ	khun
he	เขา	khǎo
she	เธอ	ther
it	มัน	man
we	เรา	rao
you (to a group)	คุณทั้งหลาย	khun tháng lǎai
you (polite, sing.)	คุณ	khun
you (polite, pl)	คุณทั้งหลาย	khun tháng lǎai
they (masc.)	เขา	khǎo
they (fem.)	เธอ	ther
Hello! (fam.)	สวัสดี!	sà-wàt-dee
Hello! (form.)	สวัสดี ครับ/ค่ะ!	sà-wàt-dee khráp/khâ
Good morning!	อรุณสวัสดิ์!	a-run sà-wàt
Good afternoon!	สวัสดีตอนบ่าย	sà-wàt-dee dtorn-bàai
Good evening!	สวัสดีตอนค่ำ	sà-wàt-dee dtorn-khâm
to say hello	ทักทาย	thák thaai
to greet (vt)	ทักทาย	thák thaai
How are you? (form.)	คุณสบายดีไหม?	khun sà-baai dee mǎi
How are you? (fam.)	สบายดีไหม?	sà-baai dee mǎi
Goodbye!	ลาก่อน!	laa gòrn
Bye!	บาย!	baai
Thank you!	ขอบคุณ!	khòrp khun
feelings	ความรู้สึก	khwaam róo sèuk
to be hungry	หิว	hǐw
to be thirsty	กระหาย	grà-hǎai
tired (adj)	เหนื่อย	nèuay
to be worried	กังวล	gang-won

to be nervous	กระวนกระวาย	grà won grà waai
hope	ความหวัง	khwaam wăng
to hope (vi, vt)	หวัง	wăng

character	นิสัย	ní-săi
modest (adj)	ถ่อมตน	thòrm dton
lazy (adj)	ขี้เกียจ	khêe gìat
generous (adj)	มีน้ำใจ	mee nám jai
talented (adj)	มีพรสวรรค์	mee phon sà-wăn

honest (adj)	ซื่อสัตย์	sêu sàt
serious (adj)	เอาจริงเอาจัง	ao jing ao jang
shy, timid (adj)	อาย	aai
sincere (adj)	จริงใจ	jing jai
coward	คนขี้ขลาด	khon khêe khlàat

to sleep (vi)	นอน	norn
dream	ความฝัน	khwaam făn
bed	เตียง	dtiang
pillow	หมอน	mŏrn

insomnia	อาการนอนไม่หลับ	aa-gaan norn mâi làp
to go to bed	ไปนอน	bpai norn
nightmare	ฝันร้าย	făn ráai
alarm clock	นาฬิกาปลุก	naa-lí-gaa bplùk

smile	รอยยิ้ม	roi yím
to smile (vi)	ยิ้ม	yím
to laugh (vi)	หัวเราะ	hŭa rór

quarrel	การทะเลาะ	gaan thá-lór
insult	คำดูถูก	kham doo thòok
resentment	ความเคียดแค้น	khwaam khîat-kháen
angry (mad)	โกรธ	gròht

7. Clothing. Personal accessories

clothes	เสื้อผ้า	sêua phâa
coat (overcoat)	เสื้อโค้ท	sêua khóht
fur coat	เสื้อโค้ทขนสัตว์	sêua khóht khŏn sàt
jacket (e.g., leather ~)	แจ็คเก็ต	jáek-gèt
raincoat (trenchcoat, etc.)	เสื้อกันฝน	sêua gan fŏn

shirt (button shirt)	เสื้อ	sêua
pants	กางเกง	gaang-gayng
suit jacket	แจ็คเก็ตสูท	jàek-gèt sòot
suit	ชุดสูท	chút sòot

| dress (frock) | ชุดเดรส | chút draet |
| skirt | กระโปรง | grà bprohng |

T-shirt	เสื้อยืด	sêua yêut
bathrobe	เสื้อคลุมอาบน้ำ	sêua khlum àap náam
pajamas	ชุดนอน	chút norn
workwear	ชุดทำงาน	chút tam ngaan
underwear	ชุดชั้นใน	chút chán nai
socks	ถุงเท้า	thǔng tháo
bra	ยกทรง	yók song
pantyhose	ถุงน่องเต็มตัว	thǔng nôrng dtem dtua
stockings (thigh highs)	ถุงน่อง	thǔng nôrng
bathing suit	ชุดว่ายน้ำ	chút wâai náam
hat	หมวก	mùak
footwear	รองเท้า	rorng tháo
boots (e.g., cowboy ~)	รองเท้าบูท	rorng tháo bòot
heel	สันรองเท้า	sôn rorng tháo
shoestring	เชือกรองเท้า	chêuak rorng tháo
shoe polish	ยาขัดรองเท้า	yaa khàt rorng tháo
cotton (n)	ฝ้าย	fâai
wool (n)	ขนสัตว์	khǒn sàt
fur (n)	ขนสัตว์	khǒn sàt
gloves	ถุงมือ	thǔng meu
mittens	ถุงมือ	thǔng meu
scarf (muffler)	ผ้าพันคอ	phâa phan khor
glasses (eyeglasses)	แว่นตา	wâen dtaa
umbrella	ร่ม	rôm
tie (necktie)	เน็คไท	nâyk-thai
handkerchief	ผ้าเช็ดหน้า	phâa chét-nâa
comb	หวี	wěe
hairbrush	แปรงหวีผม	bpraeng wěe phǒm
buckle	หัวเข็มขัด	hǔa khěm khàt
belt	เข็มขัด	khěm khàt
purse	กระเป๋าถือ	grà-bpǎo thěu
collar	คอปกเสื้อ	khor bpòk sêua
pocket	กระเป๋า	grà-bpǎo
sleeve	แขนเสื้อ	khǎen sêua
fly (on trousers)	ซิปกางเกง	síp gaang-gayng
zipper (fastener)	ซิป	síp
button	กระดุม	grà dum
to get dirty (vi)	สกปรก	sòk-gà-bpròk
stain (mark, spot)	รอยเปื้อน	roi bpêuan

8. City. Urban institutions

store	ร้านค้า	ráan kháa
shopping mall	ศูนย์การค้า	sǒon gaan kháa

supermarket	ซูเปอร์มาร์เก็ต	soo-bper-maa-gèt
shoe store	ร้านขายรองเท้า	ráan khǎai rorng táo
bookstore	ร้านขายหนังสือ	ráan khǎai nǎng-sěu
drugstore, pharmacy	ร้านขายยา	ráan khǎai yaa
bakery	ร้านขนมปัง	ráan khà-nǒm bpang
pastry shop	ร้านขนม	ráan khà-nǒm
grocery store	ร้านขายของชำ	ráan khǎai khǒrng cham
butcher shop	ร้านขายเนื้อ	ráan khǎai néua
produce store	ร้านขายผัก	ráan khǎai phàk
market	ตลาด	dtà-làat
hair salon	ร้านทำผม	ráan tham phǒm
post office	โรงไปรษณีย์	rohng bprai-sà-nee
dry cleaners	ร้านซักแห้ง	ráan sák hâeng
circus	โรงละครสัตว์	rohng lá-khon sàt
zoo	สวนสัตว์	sǔan sàt
theater	โรงละคร	rohng lá-khon
movie theater	โรงภาพยนตร์	rohng phâap-phá-yon
museum	พิพิธภัณฑ์	phí-phítha phan
library	ห้องสมุด	hôrng sà-mùt
mosque	สุเหร่า	sù-rào
synagogue	โบสถ์ยิว	bòht yiw
cathedral	อาสนวิหาร	aa sǒn wí-hǎan
temple	วิหาร	wí-hǎan
church	โบสถ์	bòht
college	วิทยาลัย	wít-thá-yaa-lai
university	มหาวิทยาลัย	má-hǎa wít-thá-yaa-lai
school	โรงเรียน	rohng rian
hotel	โรงแรม	rohng raem
bank	ธนาคาร	thá-naa-khaan
embassy	สถานทูต	sà-thǎan thôot
travel agency	บริษัททัวร์	bor-rí-sàt thua
subway	รถไฟใต้ดิน	rót fai dtâi din
hospital	โรงพยาบาล	rohng phá-yaa-baan
gas station	ปั๊มน้ำมัน	bpám náam man
parking lot	ลานจอดรถ	laan jòrt rót
ENTRANCE	ทางเข้า	thaang khâo
EXIT	ทางออก	thaang òrk
PUSH	ผลัก	phlàk
PULL	ดึง	deung
OPEN	เปิด	bpèrt
CLOSED	ปิด	bpìt
monument	อนุสาวรีย์	a-nú-sǎa-wá-ree
fortress	ป้อม	bpôrm

palace	วัง	wang
medieval (adj)	ยุคกลาง	yúk glaang
ancient (adj)	โบราณ	boh-raan
national (adj)	แห่งชาติ	hàeng châat
famous (monument, etc.)	ที่มีชื่อเสียง	thêe mee chêu-sǐang

9. Money. Finances

money	เงิน	ngern
coin	เหรียญ	rǐan
dollar	ดอลลาร์	dorn-lâa
euro	ยูโร	yoo-roh

ATM	เอทีเอ็ม	ay-thee-em
currency exchange	ร้านแลกเงิน	ráan lâek ngern
exchange rate	อัตราแลกเปลี่ยนสกุลเงิน	àt-dtraa lâek bplìan sà-gun ngern
cash	เงินสด	ngern sòt

How much?	ราคาเท่าไหร่?	raa-khaa thâo rài
to pay (vi, vt)	จ่าย	jàai
payment	การจ่ายเงิน	gaan jàai ngern
change (give the ~)	เงินทอน	ngern thorn

price	ราคา	raa-khaa
discount	ลดราคา	lót raa-khaa
cheap (adj)	ถูก	thòok
expensive (adj)	แพง	phaeng

bank	ธนาคาร	thá-naa-khaan
account	บัญชี	ban-chee
credit card	บัตรเครดิต	bàt khray-dìt
check	เช็ค	chék
to write a check	เขียนเช็ค	khǐan chék
checkbook	สมุดเช็ค	sà-mùt chék

debt	หนี้	nêe
debtor	ลูกหนี้	lôok nêe
to lend (money)	ให้ยืม	hâi yeum
to borrow (vi, vt)	ขอยืม	khǒr yeum

to rent (~ a tuxedo)	เช่า	châo
on credit (adv)	ซื้อเงินเชื่อ	séu ngern chêua
wallet	กระเป๋าเงิน	grà-bpǎo ngern
safe	ตู้เซฟ	dtôo sâyf
inheritance	มรดก	mor-rá-dòrk
fortune (wealth)	เงินจำนวนมาก	ngern jam-nuan mâak

| tax | ภาษี | phaa-sěe |
| fine | ค่าปรับ | khâa bpràp |

to fine (vt)	ปรับ	bpràp
wholesale (adj)	ขายส่ง	khǎai sòng
retail (adj)	ขายปลีก	khǎai bplèek
to insure (vt)	ประกันภัย	bprà-gan phai
insurance	การประกันภัย	gaan bprà-gan phai
capital	เงินทุน	ngern thun
turnover	การหมุนเวียน	gaan mǔn wian
stock (share)	หุ้น	hûn
profit	กำไร	gam-rai
profitable (adj)	ได้กำไร	dâai gam-rai
crisis	วิกฤติ	wí-grìt
bankruptcy	การล้มละลาย	gaan lóm lá-laai
to go bankrupt	ล้มละลาย	lóm lá-laai
accountant	นักบัญชี	nák ban-chee
salary	เงินเดือน	ngern deuan
bonus (money)	โบนัส	boh-nát

10. Transportation

bus	รถเมล์	rót may
streetcar	รถราง	rót raang
trolley bus	รถโดยสารประจำ ทางไฟฟ้า	rót doi sǎan bprà-jam thaang fai fáa
to go by ...	ไปด้วย	bpai dûay
to get on (~ the bus)	ขึ้น	khêun
to get off ...	ลง	long
stop (e.g., bus ~)	ป้าย	bpâai
terminus	ป้ายสุดท้าย	bpâai sùt tháai
schedule	ตารางเวลา	dtaa-raang way-laa
ticket	ตั๋ว	dtǔa
to be late (for ...)	ไปสาย	bpai sǎai
taxi, cab	แท็กซี่	tháek-sêe
by taxi	โดยแท็กซี่	doi tháek-sêe
taxi stand	ป้ายจอดแท็กซี่	bpâai jòrt tháek sêe
traffic	การจราจร	gaan jà-raa-jon
rush hour	ชั่วโมงเร่งด่วน	chûa mohng râyng dùan
to park (vi)	จอด	jòrt
subway	รถไฟใต้ดิน	rót fai dtâi din
station	สถานี	sà-thǎa-nee
train	รถไฟ	rót fai
train station	สถานีรถไฟ	sà-thǎa-nee rót fai
rails	รางรถไฟ	raang rót fai

| compartment | ตู้นอน | dtôo norn |
| berth | เตียง | dtiang |

airplane	เครื่องบิน	khrêuang bin
air ticket	ตั๋วเครื่องบิน	dtǔa khrêuang bin
airline	สายการบิน	sǎai gaan bin
airport	สนามบิน	sà-nǎam bin

flight (act of flying)	การบิน	gaan bin
luggage	สัมภาระ	sǎm-phaa-rá
luggage cart	รถขนสัมภาระ	rót khǒn sǎm-phaa-rá

ship	เรือ	reua
cruise ship	เรือเดินสมุทร	reua dern sà-mùt
yacht	เรือยอชต	reua yôt
boat (flat-bottomed ~)	เรือพาย	reua phaai

captain	กัปตัน	gàp dtan
cabin	ห้องพัก	hôrng phák
port (harbor)	ทาเรือ	thâa reua

bicycle	รถจักรยาน	rót jàk-grà-yaan
scooter	สกูตเตอร์	sà-góot-dtêr
motorcycle, bike	รถมอเตอร์ไซค์	rót mor-dtêr-sai
pedal	แป้นเหยียบ	bpâen yìap
pump	ปั๊ม	bpám
wheel	ล้อ	lór

automobile, car	รถยนต์	rót yon
ambulance	รถพยาบาล	rót phá-yaa-baan
truck	รถบรรทุก	rót ban-thúk
used (adj)	มือสอง	meu sǒrng
car crash	อุบัติเหตุรถชน	u-bàt hàyt rót chon
repair	การซอม	gaan sôrm

11. Food. Part 1

meat	เนื้อ	néua
chicken	ไก่	gài
duck	เป็ด	bpèt

pork	เนื้อหมู	néua mǒo
veal	เนื้อลูกวัว	néua lôok wua
lamb	เนื้อแกะ	néua gàe
beef	เนื้อวัว	néua wua

sausage (bologna, etc.)	ไส้กรอก	sâi gròrk
egg	ไข่	khài
fish	ปลา	bplaa
cheese	เนยแข็ง	noie khǎeng

sugar	น้ำตาล	nám dtaan
salt	เกลือ	gleua
rice	ข้าว	khâao
pasta (macaroni)	พาสต้า	phâat-dtâa
butter	เนย	noie
vegetable oil	น้ำมันพืช	nám man phêut
bread	ขนมปัง	khà-nǒm bpang
chocolate (n)	ช็อกโกแลต	chók-goh-láet
wine	ไวน์	wai
coffee	กาแฟ	gaa-fae
milk	นม	nom
juice	น้ำผลไม้	nám phǒn-lá-máai
beer	เบียร์	bia
tea	ชา	chaa
tomato	มะเขือเทศ	má-khěua thâyt
cucumber	แตงกวา	dtaeng-gwaa
carrot	แครอท	khae-rót
potato	มันฝรั่ง	man fà-ràng
onion	หัวหอม	hǔa hǒrm
garlic	กระเทียม	grà-thiam
cabbage	กะหล่ำปลี	gà-làm bplee
beet	บีทรูท	bee-trôot
eggplant	มะเขือยาว	má-khěua-yaao
dill	ผักชีลาว	phàk-chee-laao
lettuce	ผักกาดหอม	phàk gàat hǒrm
corn (maize)	ข้าวโพด	khâao-phôht
fruit	ผลไม้	phǒn-lá-máai
apple	แอปเปิ้ล	àep-bpêrn
pear	แพร์	phae
lemon	มะนาว	má-naao
orange	ส้ม	sôm
strawberry (garden ~)	สตรอว์เบอร์รี่	sà-dtror-ber-rêe
plum	พลัม	phlam
raspberry	ราสเบอร์รี่	râat-ber-rêe
pineapple	สับปะรด	sàp-bpà-rót
banana	กล้วย	glûay
watermelon	แตงโม	dtaeng moh
grape	องุ่น	a-ngùn
melon	เมลอน	may-lorn

12. Food. Part 2

cuisine	อาหาร	aa-hǎan
recipe	ตำราอาหาร	dtam-raa aa-hǎan

food	อาหาร	aa-hǎan
to have breakfast	ทานอาหารเช้า	thaan aa-hǎan cháo
to have lunch	ทานอาหารเที่ยง	thaan aa-hǎan thîang
to have dinner	ทานอาหารเย็น	thaan aa-hǎan yen

taste, flavor	รสชาติ	rót châat
tasty (adj)	อร่อย	à-ròi
cold (adj)	เย็น	yen
hot (adj)	ร้อน	rórn
sweet (sugary)	หวาน	wǎan
salty (adj)	เค็ม	khem

sandwich (bread)	แซนด์วิช	saen-wít
side dish	เครื่องเคียง	khrêuang khiang
filling (for cake, pie)	ไส้ในขนม	sâi nai khà-nǒm
sauce	ซอส	sós
piece (of cake, pie)	ชิ้น	chín

diet	อาหารพิเศษ	aa-hǎan phí-sàyt
vitamin	วิตามิน	wí-dtaa-min
calorie	แคลอรี่	khae-lor-rêe
vegetarian (n)	คนกินเจ	khon gin jay

restaurant	ร้านอาหาร	ráan aa-hǎan
coffee house	ร้านกาแฟ	ráan gaa-fae
appetite	ความอยากอาหาร	kwaam yàak aa hǎan
Enjoy your meal!	กินให้อร่อย!	gin hâi a-ròi

waiter	คนเสิร์ฟชาย	khon sèrf chaai
waitress	คนเสิร์ฟหญิง	khon sèrf yǐng
bartender	บาร์เทนเดอร์	baa-thayn-dêr
menu	เมนู	may-noo

spoon	ช้อน	chórn
knife	มีด	mêet
fork	ส้อม	sôrm
cup (e.g., coffee ~)	แก้ว	gâew

plate (dinner ~)	จาน	jaan
saucer	จานรอง	jaan rorng
napkin (on table)	ผ้าเช็ดปาก	phâa chét bpàak
toothpick	ไม้จิ้มฟัน	máai jîm fan

to order (meal)	สั่ง	sàng
course, dish	มื้ออาหาร	méu aa-hǎan
portion	ส่วน	sùan
appetizer	ของกินเล่น	khǒrng gin lâyn
salad	สลัด	sà-làt
soup	ซุป	súp

| dessert | ของหวาน | khǒrng wǎan |
| jam (whole fruit jam) | แยม | yaem |

ice-cream	ไอศกรีม	ai-sà-greem
check	คิดเงิน	khít ngern
to pay the check	จ่ายค่าอาหาร	jàai khâa aa hăan
tip	เงินทิป	ngern thíp

13. House. Apartment. Part 1

house	บ้าน	bâan
country house	บ้านสไตล์คันทรี่	bâan sà-dtai khan trêe
villa (seaside ~)	คฤหาสน์	khá-réu-hàat
floor, story	ชั้น	chán
entrance	ทางเข้า	thaang khâo
wall	ฝาผนัง	făa phà-năng
roof	หลังคา	lăng khaa
chimney	ปล่องควัน	bplòrng khwan
attic (storage place)	ห้องใต้หลังคา	hôrng dtâi lăng-khaa
window	หน้าต่าง	nâa dtàang
window ledge	ชั้นติดผนัง	chán dtìt phà-năng
	ใต้หน้าต่าง	dtâi nâa dtàang
balcony	ระเบียง	rá-biang
stairs (stairway)	บันได	ban-dai
mailbox	ตู้จดหมาย	dtôo jòt măai
garbage can	ถังขยะ	thăng khà-yà
elevator	ลิฟต์	líf
electricity	ไฟฟ้า	fai fáa
light bulb	หลอดไฟฟ้า	lòrt fai fáa
switch	ปุ่มปิดเปิดไฟ	bpùm bpìt bpèrt fai
wall socket	เต้าเสียบปลั๊กไฟ	dtâo sìap bplák fai
fuse	ฟิวส์	fiw
door	ประตู	bprà-dtoo
handle, doorknob	ลูกบิดประตู	lôok bìt bprà-dtoo
key	ลูกกุญแจ	lôok gun-jae
doormat	ที่เช็ดเท้า	thêe chét tháo
door lock	แม่กุญแจ	mâe gun-jae
doorbell	กระดิ่งประตู	grà-dìng bprà-dtoo
knock (at the door)	เสียงเคาะ	sĭang khór
to knock (vi)	เคาะ	khór
peephole	ช่องตาแมว	chôrng dtaa maew
yard	สนาม	sà-năam
garden	สวน	sŭan
swimming pool	สระว่ายน้ำ	sà wâai náam
gym (home gym)	โรงยิม	rohng-yim
tennis court	สนามเทนนิส	sà-năam then-nít

garage	โรงรถ	rohng rót
private property	ทรัพย์สินส่วนบุคคล	sáp sĭn sùan bùk-khon
warning sign	ป้ายเตือน	bpâai dteuan
security	ผู้รักษา ความปลอดภัย	phôo rák-săa khwaam bplòrt phai
security guard	ยาม	yaam

renovations	การซ่อมแซม	gaan sôrm saem
to renovate (vt)	ซ่อมแซม	sôrm saem
to put in order	สะสาง	sà-săang
to paint (~ a wall)	ทาสี	thaa sĕe
wallpaper	วอลเปเปอร์	worn-bpay-bper
to varnish (vt)	เคลือบ	khlêuap

pipe	ท่อ	thôr
tools	เครื่องมือ	khrêuang meu
basement	ชั้นใต้ดิน	chán dtâi din
sewerage (system)	ระบบท่อน้ำทิ้ง	rá-bòp thôr náam thíng

14. House. Apartment. Part 2

apartment	อพาร์ตเมนต์	a-phâat-mayn
room	ห้อง	hôrng
bedroom	ห้องนอน	hôrng norn
dining room	ห้องรับประทานอาหาร	hôrng ráp bprà-thaan aa-hăan

living room	ห้องนั่งเล่น	hôrng nâng lên
study (home office)	ห้องทำงาน	hôrng tham ngaan
entry room	ห้องเข้า	hôrng khâo
bathroom (room with a bath or shower)	ห้องน้ำ	hôrng náam
half bath	ห้องส้วม	hôrng sûam

| floor | พื้น | phéun |
| ceiling | เพดาน | phay-daan |

to dust (vt)	ปัดกวาด	bpàt gwàat
vacuum cleaner	เครื่องดูดฝุ่น	khrêuang dòot fùn
to vacuum (vt)	ดูดฝุ่น	dòot fùn

mop	ไม้ถูพื้น	mái thŏo phéun
dust cloth	ผ้าเช็ดพื้น	phâa chét phéun
short broom	ไม้กวาดสั้น	máai gwàat sân
dustpan	ที่ตักผง	têe dtàk phŏng

furniture	เครื่องเรือน	khrêuang reuan
table	โต๊ะ	dtó
chair	เก้าอี้	gâo-êe
armchair	เก้าอี้เท้าแขน	gâo-êe tháo khăen

bookcase	ตู้หนังสือ	dtôo năng-sĕu
shelf	ชั้นวาง	chán waang
wardrobe	ตู้เสื้อผ้า	dtôo sêua phâa

mirror	กระจก	grà-jòk
carpet	พรม	phrom
fireplace	เตาผิง	dtao phĭng
drapes	ผ้าแขวน	phâa khwăen
table lamp	โคมไฟตั้งโต๊ะ	khohm fai dtâng dtó
chandelier	โคมระยา	khohm rá-yáa

kitchen	ห้องครัว	hôrng khrua
gas stove (range)	เตาแก๊ส	dtao gàet
electric stove	เตาไฟฟ้า	dtao fai-fáa
microwave oven	เตาอบไมโครเวฟ	dtao òp mai-khroh-we p

refrigerator	ตู้เย็น	dtôo yen
freezer	ตู้แช่แข็ง	dtôo châe khăeng
dishwasher	เครื่องล้างจาน	khrêuang láang jaan
faucet	ก๊อกน้ำ	gòk náam

meat grinder	เครื่องบดเนื้อ	khrêuang bòt néua
juicer	เครื่องคั้น น้ำผลไม้	khrêuang khán náam phŏn-lá-mái
toaster	เครื่องปิ้ง ขนมปัง	khrêuang bpîng khà-nŏm bpang
mixer	เครื่องปั่น	khrêuang bpàn

coffee machine	เครื่องชงกาแฟ	khrêuang chong gaa-fae
kettle	กาน้ำ	gaa náam
teapot	กาน้ำชา	gaa náam chaa

TV set	ทีวี	thee-wee
VCR (video recorder)	เครื่องบันทึก วิดีโอ	khrêuang ban-théuk wí-dee-oh
iron (e.g., steam ~)	เตารีด	dtao rêet
telephone	โทรศัพท์	thoh-rá-sàp

15. Professions. Social status

director	ผู้อำนวยการ	phôo am-nuay gaan
superior	ผู้บังคับบัญชา	phôo bang-kháp ban-chaa
president	ประธานาธิปดี	bprà-thaa-naa-thí-bor-dee
assistant	ผู้ช่วย	phôo chûay
secretary	เลขา	lay-khăa

owner, proprietor	เจ้าของ	jâo khŏrng
partner	หุ้นส่วน	hûn sùan
stockholder	ผู้ถือหุ้น	phôo thĕu hûn
businessman	นักธุรกิจ	nák thú-rá-gìt

millionaire	เศรษฐีเงินล้าน	sàyt-thĕe ngern láan
billionaire	มหาเศรษฐี	má-hăa sàyt-thĕe
actor	นักแสดงชาย	nák sà-daeng chaai
architect	สถาปนิก	sà-thăa-bpà-ník
banker	พนักงาน	phá-nák ngaan
	ธนาคาร	thá-naa-khaan
broker	นายหน้า	naai nâa
veterinarian	สัตวแพทย์	sàt phâet
doctor	แพทย	phâet
chambermaid	แมบาน	mâe bâan
designer	นักออกแบบ	nák òrk bàep
correspondent	ผู้สื่อขาว	phôo sèu khàao
delivery man	คนสงของ	khon sòng khŏrng
electrician	ช่างไฟฟ้า	châang fai-fáa
musician	นักดนตรี	nák don-dtree
babysitter	พี่เลี้ยงเด็ก	phêe líang dèk
hairdresser	ชางทำผม	châang tham phŏm
herder, shepherd	คนเลี้ยงปศุสัตว์	khon líang bpà-sù-sàt
singer (masc.)	นักร้องชาย	nák rórng chaai
translator	นักแปล	nák bplae
writer	นักเขียน	nák khĭan
carpenter	ชางไม	châang máai
cook	คนครัว	khon khrua
fireman	เจ้าหน้าที่ดับเพลิง	jâo nâa-thêe dàp phlerng
police officer	เจาหนาที่ตำรวจ	jâo nâa-thêe dtam-rùat
mailman	บุรุษไปรษณีย	bù-rùt bprai-sà-nee
programmer	นักเขียนโปรแกรม	nák khĭan bproh-graem
salesman (store staff)	คนขายของ	khon khăai khŏrng
worker	คนงาน	khon ngaan
gardener	ชาวสวน	chaao sŭan
plumber	ชางประปา	châang bprà-bpaa
dentist	ทันตแพทย	than-dtà phâet
flight attendant (fem.)	พนักงนตอนรับ	phá-nák ngaan dtôrn ráp
	บนเครื่องบิน	bon khrêuang bin
dancer (masc.)	นักเต้นชาย	nák dtên chaai
bodyguard	ผูคุมกัน	phôo khúm gan
scientist	นักวิทยาศาสตร	nák wít-thá-yaa sàat
schoolteacher	อาจารย	aa-jaan
farmer	ชาวนา	chaao naa
surgeon	ศัลยแพทย	săn-yá-phâet
miner	คูนงานเหมือง	khon ngaan mĕuang
chef (kitchen chef)	กุก	gúk
driver	คนขับ	khon khàp

16. Sport

kind of sports	ประเภทกีฬา	bprà-phâyt gee-laa
soccer	ฟุตบอล	fút bon
hockey	ฮอกกี้	hôk-gêe
basketball	บาสเก็ตบอล	bàat-gèt-bon
baseball	เบสบอล	bàyt-bon
volleyball	วอลเลย์บอล	won-lây-bon
boxing	การชกมวย	gaan chók muay
wrestling	การมวยปล้ำ	gaan muay bplâm
tennis	เทนนิส	then-nít
swimming	กีฬาว่ายน้ำ	gee-laa wâai náam
chess	หมากรุก	màak rúk
running	การวิ่ง	gaan wîng
athletics	กรีฑา	gree thaa
figure skating	สเก็ตลีลา	sà-gèt lee-laa
cycling	การแข่งจักรยาน	gaan khàeng jàk-grà-yaan
billiards	บิลเลียด	bin-lîat
bodybuilding	การเพาะกาย	gaan phór gaai
golf	กอล์ฟ	góf
scuba diving	การดำน้ำ	gaan dam náam
sailing	การแล่นเรือใบ	gaan lâen reua bai
archery	การยิงธนู	gaan ying thá-noo
period, half	ครึ่ง	khrêung
half-time	ช่วงพักครึ่ง	chûang phák khrêung
tie	เสมอ	sà-měr
to tie (vi)	เสมอ	sà-měr
treadmill	ลู่วิ่งออกกำลังกาย	lôo wîng òk gam-lang gaai
player	ผู้เล่น	phôo lên
substitute	ผู้เล่นสำรอง	phôo lên săm-rorng
substitutes bench	ซุ้มม้านั่ง	súm máa nâng
	ตัวสำรอง	dtua săm-rorng
match	เกมการแข่ง	gaym gaan khàeng
goal	ประตู	bprà-dtoo
goalkeeper	ผู้รักษาประตู	phôo rák-săa bprà-dtoo
goal (score)	ประตู	bprà-dtoo
Olympic Games	กีฬาโอลิมปิก	gee-laa oh-lim-bpìk
to set a record	ทำสถิติ	tham sà-thì-dtì
final	รอบสุดท้าย	rôrp sùt tháai
champion	แชมเปี้ยน	chaem-bpîan
championship	ชิงแชมป์	ching chaem
winner	ผู้ชนะ	phôo chá-ná
victory	ชัยชนะ	chai chá-ná

to win (vi)	ชนะ	chá-ná
to lose (not win)	แพ้	pháe
medal	เหรียญรางวัล	rǐan raang-wan

first place	อันดับที่หนึ่ง	an-dàp thêe nèung
second place	อันดับที่สอง	an-dàp thêe sǒrng
third place	อันดับที่สาม	an-dàp thêe sǎam

stadium	สนาม	sà-nǎam
fan, supporter	แฟน	faen
trainer, coach	โค้ช	khóht
training	การฝึกหัด	gaan fèuk hàt

17. Foreign languages. Orthography

language	ภาษา	phaa-sǎa
to study (vt)	เรียน	rian
pronunciation	การออกเสียง	gaan òrk sǐang
accent	สำเนียง	sǎm-niang

noun	นาม	naam
adjective	คำคุณศัพท์	kham khun-ná-sàp
verb	กริยา	grì-yaa
adverb	คำวิเศษณ์	kham wí-sàyt

pronoun	คำสรรพนาม	kham sàp-phá-naam
interjection	คำอุทาน	kham u-thaan
preposition	คำบุพบท	kham bùp-phá-bòt

root	รากศัพท์	râak sàp
ending	คำลงท้าย	kham long tháai
prefix	คำนำหน้า	kham nam nâa
syllable	พยางค์	phá-yaang
suffix	คำเสริมท้าย	kham sěrm tháai

stress mark	เครื่องหมายเน้น	khrêuang mǎai náyn
period, dot	จุด	jùt
comma	จุลภาค	jun-lá-phâak
colon	ทวิภาค	thá-wí phâak
ellipsis	การละไว้	gaan lá wái

question	คำถาม	kham thǎam
question mark	เครื่องหมายปรัศนี	khrêuang mǎai bpràt-nee
exclamation point	เครื่องหมายอัศเจรีย์	khrêuang mǎai àt-sà-jay-ree

in quotation marks	ในอัญประกาศ	nai an-yá-bprà-gàat
in parenthesis	ในวงเล็บ	nai wong lép
letter	ตัวอักษร	dtua àk-sǒn
capital letter	อักษรตัวใหญ่	àk-sǒn dtua yài

sentence	ประโยค	bprà-yòhk
group of words	กลุ่มคำ	glùm kham
expression	วลี	wá-lee

subject	ภาคประธาน	phâak bprà-thaan
predicate	ภาคแสดง	phâak sà-daeng
line	บรรทัด	ban-thát
paragraph	วรรค	wák

synonym	คำพ้องความหมาย	kham phóng khwaam mǎai
antonym	คำตรงกันข้าม	kham dtrorng gan khâam
exception	ข้อยกเว้น	khôr yok-wâyn
to underline (vt)	ขีดเส้นใต้	khèet sên dtâi

rules	กฎ	gòt
grammar	ไวยากรณ์	wai-yaa-gon
vocabulary	คำศัพท์	kham sàp
phonetics	การออกเสียง	gaan òrk sǐang
alphabet	ตัวอักษร	dtua àk-sǒn

textbook	หนังสือเรียน	nǎng-sěu rian
dictionary	พจนานุกรม	phót-jà-naa-nú-grom
phrasebook	เฟรสบุก	frayt bùk

word	คำ	kham
meaning	ความหมาย	khwaam mǎai
memory	ความทรงจำ	khwaam song jam

18. The Earth. Geography

the Earth	โลก	lôhk
the globe (the Earth)	ลูกโลก	lôok lôhk
planet	ดาวเคราะห์	daao khrór

geography	ภูมิศาสตร์	phoo-mí-sàat
nature	ธรรมชาติ	tham-má-châat
map	แผนที่	phǎen thêe
atlas	หนังสือแผนที่โลก	nǎng-sěu phǎen thêe lôhk

in the north	ที่ภาคเหนือ	thêe phâak něua
in the south	ที่ภาคใต้	thêe phâak dtâi
in the west	ที่ภาคตะวันตก	thêe phâak dtà-wan dtòk
in the east	ที่ภาคตะวันออก	thêe phâak dtà-wan òrk

sea	ทะเล	thá-lay
ocean	มหาสมุทร	má-hǎa sà-mùt
gulf (bay)	อ่าว	àao
straits	ช่องแคบ	chôrng khâep
continent (mainland)	ทวีป	thá-wêep
island	เกาะ	gòr

peninsula	คาบสมุทร	khâap sà-mùt
archipelago	หมูเกาะ	mòo gòr
harbor	ท่าเรือ	thâa reua
coral reef	แนวปะการัง	naew bpà-gaa-rang
shore	ชายฝั่ง	chaai fàng
coast	ชายฝั่ง	chaai fàng
flow (flood tide)	น้ำขึ้น	náam khêun
ebb (ebb tide)	น้ำลง	náam long
latitude	เส้นรุ้ง	sên rúng
longitude	เส้นแวง	sên waeng
parallel	เส้นขนาน	sên khà-nǎan
equator	เส้นศูนย์สูตร	sên sǒon sòot
sky	ท้องฟ้า	thórng fáa
horizon	ขอบฟ้า	khòrp fáa
atmosphere	บรรยากาศ	ban-yaa-gàat
mountain	ภูเขา	phoo khǎo
summit, top	ยอดเขา	yôrt khǎo
cliff	หน้าผา	nâa phǎa
hill	เนินเขา	nern khǎo
volcano	ภูเขาไฟ	phoo khǎo fai
glacier	ธารน้ำแข็ง	thaan náam khǎeng
waterfall	น้ำตก	nám dtòk
plain	ที่ราบ	thêe râap
river	แม่น้ำ	mâe náam
spring (natural source)	แหล่งน้ำแร่	làeng náam râe
bank (of river)	ฝั่งแม่น้ำ	fàng mâe náam
downstream (adv)	ตามกระแสน้ำ	dtaam grà-sǎe náam
upstream (adv)	ทวนน้ำ	thuan náam
lake	ทะเลสาบ	thá-lay sàap
dam	เขื่อน	khèuan
canal	คลอง	khlorng
swamp (marshland)	บึง	beung
ice	น้ำแข็ง	nám khǎeng

19. Countries of the world. Part 1

Europe	ยุโรป	yú-ròhp
European Union	สหภาพยุโรป	sà-hà phâap yú-rôhp
European (n)	คนยุโรป	khon yú-rôhp
European (adj)	ยุโรป	yú-rôhp
Austria	ประเทศออสเตรีย	bprà-thâyt òt-dtria
Great Britain	บริเตนใหญ่	brì-dtayn yài

England	ประเทศอังกฤษ	bprà-thâyt ang-grìt
Belgium	ประเทศเบลเยียม	bprà-thâyt bayn-yiam
Germany	ประเทศเยอรมนี	bprà-thâyt yer-rá-ma-nee
Netherlands	ประเทศเนเธอร์แลนด์	bprà-thâyt nay-ther-laen
Holland	ประเทศฮอลแลนด	bprà-thâyt hon-laen
Greece	ประเทศกรีซ	bprà-thâyt grèet
Denmark	ประเทศเดนมาร์ก	bprà-thâyt dayn-màak
Ireland	ประเทศไอรแลนด์	bprà-thâyt ai-laen
Iceland	ประเทศไอซ์แลนด์	bprà-thâyt ai-laen
Spain	ประเทศสเปน	bprà-thâyt sà-bpayn
Italy	ประเทศอิตาลี	bprà-thâyt i-dtaa-lee
Cyprus	ประเทศไซปรัส	bprà-thâyt sai-bpràt
Malta	ประเทศมอลตา	bprà-thâyt mon-dtaa
Norway	ประเทศนอร์เวย์	bprà-thâyt nor-way
Portugal	ประเทศโปรตุเกส	bprà-thâyt bproh-dtù-gàyt
Finland	ประเทศฟินแลนด	bprà-thâyt fin-laen
France	ประเทศฝรั่งเศส	bprà-thâyt fà-ràng-sàyt
Sweden	ประเทศสวีเดน	bprà-thâyt sà-wĕe-dayn
Switzerland	ประเทศสวิตเซอร์แลนด์	bprà-thâyt sà-wìt-sêr-laen
Scotland	ประเทศสก็อตแลนด	bprà-thâyt sà-gòt-laen
Vatican	นครรัฐวาติกัน	ná-khon rát waa-dtì-gan
Liechtenstein	ประเทศ ลิกเตนสไตน์	bprà-thâyt lík-tay-ná-sà-dtai
Luxembourg	ประเทศลักเซมเบิร์ก	bprà-thâyt lák-saym-bèrk
Monaco	ประเทศโมนาโก	bprà-thâyt moh-naa-goh
Albania	ประเทศแอลเบเนีย	bprà-thâyt aen-bay-nia
Bulgaria	ประเทศบัลแกเรีย	bprà-thâyt ban-gae-ria
Hungary	ประเทศฮังการี	bprà-thâyt hang-gaa-ree
Latvia	ประเทศลัตเวีย	bprà-thâyt lát-wia
Lithuania	ประเทศลิทัวเนีย	bprà-thâyt lí-thua-nia
Poland	ประเทศโปแลนด์	bprà-thâyt bpoh-laen
Romania	ประเทศโรมาเนีย	bprà-thâyt roh-maa-nia
Serbia	ประเทศเซอร์เบีย	bprà-thâyt sêr-bia
Slovakia	ประเทศสโลวาเกีย	bprà-thâyt sà-loh-waa-gia
Croatia	ประเทศโครเอเชีย	bprà-thâyt khroh-ay-chia
Czech Republic	ประเทศเช็กเกีย	bprà-thâyt chék-gia
Estonia	ประเทศเอสโตเนีย	bprà-thâyt àyt-dtoh-nia
Bosnia and Herzegovina	ประเทศบอสเนีย และเฮอรเซไกวินา	bprà-thâyt bòt-nia láe her-say-goh-wí-naa
Macedonia (Republic of ~)	ประเทศมาซิโดเนีย	bprà-thâyt maa-sí-doh-nia
Slovenia	ประเทศสโลวีเนีย	bprà-thâyt sà-loh-wee-nia
Montenegro	ประเทศ มอนเตเนโกร	bprà-thâyt mon-dtay-nay-groh
Belarus	ประเทศเบลารุส	bprà-thâyt blao-rút

Moldova, Moldavia	ประเทศมอลโดวา	bprà-thâyt mon-doh-waa
Russia	ประเทศรัสเซีย	bprà-thâyt rát-sia
Ukraine	ประเทศยูเครน	bprà-thâyt yoo-khrayn

20. Countries of the world. Part 2

Asia	เอเชีย	ay-chia
Vietnam	ประเทศเวียดนาม	bprà-thâyt wîat-naam
India	ประเทศอินเดีย	bprà-thâyt in-dia
Israel	ประเทศอิสราเอล	bprà-thâyt ìt-sà-rǎa-ayn
China	ประเทศจีน	bprà-thâyt jeen
Lebanon	ประเทศเลบานอน	bprà-thâyt lay-baa-non
Mongolia	ประเทศมองโกเลีย	bprà-thâyt mong-goh-lia
Malaysia	ประเทศมาเลเซีย	bprà-thâyt maa-lay-sia
Pakistan	ประเทศ ปากีสถาน	bprà-thâyt bpaa-gèet-thǎan
Saudi Arabia	ประเทศ ซาอุดิอาระเบีย	bprà-thâyt saa-u-dì aa-ra--bia
Thailand	ประเทศไทย	bprà-tâyt thai
Taiwan	ไต้หวัน	dtâi-wǎn
Turkey	ประเทศตุรกี	bprà-thâyt dtù-rá-gee
Japan	ประเทศญี่ปุ่น	bprà-thâyt yêe-bpùn
Afghanistan	ประเทศอัฟกานิสถาน	bprà-thâyt àf-gaa-nít-thǎan
Bangladesh	ประเทศ บังคลาเทศ	bprà-thâyt bang-khlaa-thâyt
Indonesia	ประเทศอินโดนีเซีย	bprà-thâyt in-doh-nee-sia
Jordan	ประเทศจอร์แดน	bprà-thâyt jor-daen
Iraq	ประเทศอิรัก	bprà-thâyt i-rák
Iran	ประเทศอิหราน	bprà-thâyt i-ràan
Cambodia	ประเทศกัมพูชา	bprà-thâyt gam-phoo-chaa
Kuwait	ประเทศคูเวต	bprà-thâyt khoo-wâyt
Laos	ประเทศลาว	bprà-thâyt laao
Myanmar	ประเทศเมียนมาร์	bprà-thâyt mian-maa
Nepal	ประเทศเนปาล	bprà-thâyt nay-bpaan
United Arab Emirates	สหรัฐอาหรับเอมิเรตส์	sà-hà-rát aa-ràp ay-mí-râyt
Syria	ประเทศซีเรีย	bprà-thâyt see-ria
Palestine	ปาเลสไตน์	bpaa-lâyt-dtai
South Korea	เกาหลีใต้	gao-lěe dtâi
North Korea	เกาหลีเหนือ	gao-lěe něua
United States of America	สหรัฐอเมริกา	sà-hà-rát a-may-rí-gaa
Canada	ประเทศแคนาดา	bprà-thâyt khae-naa-daa
Mexico	ประเทศเม็กซิโก	bprà-thâyt mék-sí-goh
Argentina	ประเทศอาร์เจนตินา	bprà-thâyt aa-jayn-dtì-naa
Brazil	ประเทศบราซิล	bprà-thâyt braa-sin

Colombia	ประเทศโคลัมเบีย	bprà-thâyt khoh-lam-bia
Cuba	ประเทศคิวบา	bprà-thâyt khiw-baa
Chile	ประเทศชิลี	bprà-thâyt chí-lee
Venezuela	ประเทศเวเนซุเอลา	bprà-thâyt way-nay-sú-ay-laa
Ecuador	ประเทศเอกวาดอร์	bprà-thâyt ay-gwaa-dor
The Bahamas	ประเทศบาฮามาส	bprà-thâyt baa-haa-mâat
Panama	ประเทศปานามา	bprà-thâyt bpaa-naa-maa
Egypt	ประเทศอียิปต์	bprà-thâyt bprà-thâyt ee-yíp
Morocco	ประเทศมอร์อคโค	bprà-thâyt mor-rók-khoh
Tunisia	ประเทศตูนิเซีย	bprà-thâyt dtoo-ní-sia
Kenya	ประเทศเคนย่า	bprà-thâyt khayn-yâa
Libya	ประเทศลิเบีย	bprà-thâyt lí-bia
South Africa	ประเทศแอฟริกาใต้	bprà-thâyt àef-rí-gaa dtâi
Australia	ประเทศออสเตรเลีย	bprà-thâyt òt-dtray-lia
New Zealand	ประเทศนิวซีแลนด์	bprà-thâyt niw-see-laen

21. Weather. Natural disasters

weather	สภาพอากาศ	sà-phâap aa-gàat
weather forecast	พยากรณ์ สภาพอากาศ	phá-yaa-gon sà-phâap aa-gàat
temperature	อุณหภูมิ	un-hà-phoom
thermometer	ปรอทวัดอุณหภูมิ	bpà-ròrt wát un-hà-phoom
barometer	เครื่องวัดความดัน บรรยากาศ	khrêuang wát khwaam dan ban-yaa-gàat
sun	ดวงอาทิตย์	duang aa-thít
to shine (vi)	สองแสง	sòrng sǎeng
sunny (day)	มีแสงแดด	mee sǎeng dàet
to come up (vi)	ขึ้น	khêun
to set (vi)	ตก	dtòk
rain	ฝน	fǒn
it's raining	ฝนตก	fǒn dtòk
pouring rain	ฝนตกหนัก	fǒn dtòk nàk
rain cloud	เมฆฝน	mâyk fǒn
puddle	หลุมน้ำ	lòm nám
to get wet (in rain)	เปียก	bpìak
thunderstorm	พายุฟ้าคะนอง	phaa-yú fáa khá-nong
lightning (~ strike)	ฟ้าผ่า	fáa phàa
to flash (vi)	แลบ	lâep
thunder	ฟ้าคะนอง	fáa khá-norng
it's thundering	มีฟ้าร้อง	mee fáa rórng
hail	ลูกเห็บ	lôok hèp
it's hailing	มีลูกเห็บตก	mee lôok hèp dtòk

heat (extreme ~)	ความร้อน	khwaam rórn
it's hot	มันร้อน	man rórn
it's warm	มันอุ่น	man ùn
it's cold	อากาศเย็น	aa-gàat yen

fog (mist)	หมอก	mòrk
foggy	หมอกจัด	mòrk jàt
cloud	เมฆ	mâyk
cloudy (adj)	มีเมฆมาก	mee mâyk mâak
humidity	ความชื้น	khwaam chéun

snow	หิมะ	hì-má
it's snowing	หิมะตก	hì-má dtòk
frost (severe ~, freezing cold)	ความหนาวๆ	kwaam nǎao nǎao
below zero (adv)	ต่ำกว่าศูนย์องศา	dtàm gwàa sǒon ong-sǎa
hoarfrost	น้ำค้างแข็ง	náam kháang khǎeng

bad weather	อากาศไม่ดี	aa-gàat mâi dee
disaster	ความหายนะ	khwaam hǎa-yá-ná
flood, inundation	น้ำท่วม	nám thûam
avalanche	หิมะถล่ม	hì-má thà-lòm
earthquake	แผ่นดินไหว	phàen din wǎi

tremor, shoke	ไหว	wǎi
epicenter	จุดเหนือศูนย์แผ่นดินไหว	jùt něua sǒon phàen din wǎi
eruption	ภูเขาไฟระเบิด	phoo khǎo fai rá-bèrt
lava	ลาวา	laa-waa

tornado	พายุทอร์เนโด	phaa-yú thor-nay-doh
twister	พายุหมุน	phaa-yú mǔn
hurricane	พายุเฮอร์ริเคน	phaa-yú her-rí-khayn
tsunami	คลื่นสึนามิ	khlêun sèu-naa-mí
cyclone	พายุไซโคลน	phaa-yú sai-khlohn

22. Animals. Part 1

animal	สัตว์	sàt
predator	สัตว์กินเนื้อ	sàt gin néua

tiger	เสือ	sěua
lion	สิงโต	sǐng dtoh
wolf	หมาป่า	mǎa bpàa
fox	หมาจิ้งจอก	mǎa jîng-jòk
jaguar	เสือจากัวร์	sěua jaa-gua

lynx	แมวป่า	maew bpàa
coyote	โคโยตี้	khoh-yoh-dtêe
jackal	หมาจิ้งจอกทอง	mǎa jîng-jòk thorng

hyena	ไฮยีนา	hai-yee-naa
squirrel	กระรอก	grà rôk
hedgehog	เมน	mâyn
rabbit	กระต่าย	grà-dtàai
raccoon	แร็คคูน	ráek khoon

hamster	หนูแฮมสเตอร์	nŏo haem-sà-dtêr
mole	ตุ่น	dtùn
mouse	หนู	nŏo
rat	หนู	nŏo
bat	ค้างคาว	kháang khaao

beaver	บีเวอร์	bee-wer
horse	ม้า	máa
deer	กวาง	gwaang
camel	อูฐ	òot
zebra	ม้าลาย	máa laai

whale	วาฬ	waan
seal	แมวน้ำ	maew náam
walrus	ช้างน้ำ	cháang náam
dolphin	โลมา	loh-maa

bear	หมี	měe
monkey	ลิง	ling
elephant	ช้าง	cháang

| rhinoceros | แรด | râet |
| giraffe | ยีราฟ | yee-râaf |

| hippopotamus | ฮิปโปโปเตมัส | híp-bpoh-bpoh-dtay-mát |
| kangaroo | จิงโจ้ | jing-jôh |

| cat | แมวตัวเมีย | maew dtua mia |
| dog | สุนัข | sù-nák |

| cow | วัว | wua |
| bull | กระทิง | grà-thing |

| sheep (ewe) | แกะตัวเมีย | gàe dtua mia |
| goat | แพะตัวเมีย | pháe dtua mia |

| donkey | ลา | laa |
| pig, hog | หมู | mŏo |

| hen (chicken) | ไก่ตัวเมีย | gài dtua mia |
| rooster | ไก่ตัวผู้ | gài dtua phôo |

duck	เป็ดตัวเมีย	bpèt dtua mia
goose	ห่าน	hàan
turkey (hen)	ไก่งวงตัวเมีย	gài nguang dtua mia
sheepdog	สุนัขเลี้ยงแกะ	sù-nák líang gàe

23. Animals. Part 2

bird	นก	nók
pigeon	นกพิราบ	nók phí-râap
sparrow	นกกระจิบ	nók grà-jìp
tit (great tit)	นกติ๊ด	nók dtít
magpie	นกสาลิกา	nók sǎa-lí gaa
eagle	นกอินทรี	nók in-see
hawk	นกเหยี่ยว	nók yìeow
falcon	นกเหยี่ยว	nók yìeow
swan	นกหงส์	nók hǒng
crane	นกกระเรียน	nók grà rian
stork	นกกระสา	nók grà-sǎa
parrot	นกแก้ว	nók gâew
peacock	นกยูง	nók yoong
ostrich	นกกระจอกเทศ	nók grà-jòrk-thâyt
heron	นกยาง	nók yaang
nightingale	นกไนติงเกล	nók-nai-dting-gayn
swallow	นกนางแอ่น	nók naang-àen
woodpecker	นกหัวขวาน	nók hǔa khwǎan
cuckoo	นกดุเหวา	nók dù hǎy wâa
owl	นกฮูก	nók hôok
penguin	นกเพนุกวิน	nók phayn-gwin
tuna	ปลาทูนา	bplaa thoo-nâa
trout	ปลาเทราท์	bplaa thrau
eel	ปลาไหล	bplaa lǎi
shark	ปลาฉลาม	bplaa chà-lǎam
crab	ปู	bpoo
jellyfish	แมงกะพรุน	maeng gà-phrun
octopus	ปลาหมึก	bplaa mèuk
starfish	ปลาดาว	bplaa daao
sea urchin	หอยเม่น	hǒi mâyn
seahorse	ม้าน้ำ	máa nám
shrimp	กุ้ง	gûng
snake	งู	ngoo
viper	งูแมวเซา	ngoo maew sao
lizard	กิ้งกา	gîng-gàa
iguana	อีกัวนา	ee gua naa
chameleon	กิ้งกาคามิเลียน	gîng-gàa khaa-mí-lian
scorpion	แมงป่อง	maeng bpòrng
turtle	เต่า	dtào
frog	กบ	gòp
crocodile	จระเข้	jor-rá-khây

insect, bug	แมลง	má-laeng
butterfly	ผีเสื้อ	phĕe sêua
ant	มด	mót
fly	แมลงวัน	má-laeng wan

mosquito	ยุง	yung
beetle	แมลงปีกแข็ง	má-laeng bpèek khăeng
bee	ผึ้ง	phêung
spider	แมงมุม	maeng mum

24. Trees. Plants

tree	ต้นไม้	dtôn máai
birch	ต้นเบิร์ช	dtôn bèrt
oak	ต้นโอ๊ค	dtôn óhk
linden tree	ต้นไม้ดอกเหลือง	dtôn máai dòrk lĕuang
aspen	ต้นแอสเพน	dtôn ae sà-phayn

maple	ต้นเมเปิ้ล	dtôn may bpêrn
spruce	ต้นเฟอร์	dtôn fer
pine	ต้นเกี๊ยะ	dtôn gía
cedar	ตนซีดาร์	dtôn-see-daa

poplar	ต้นปอปลาร์	dtôn bpor-bplaa
rowan	ต้นโรวัน	dtôn-roh-waen
beech	ต้นบีช	dtôn bèet
elm	ตนเอล์ม	dtôn elm

ash (tree)	ต้นแอช	dtôn aesh
chestnut	ต้นเกาลัด	dtôn gao lát
palm tree	ตนปูลม	dtôn bpaam
bush	พุ่มไม้	phûm máai

mushroom	เห็ด	hèt
poisonous mushroom	เห็ดมีพิษ	hèt mee pít
cep (Boletus edulis)	เห็ดพอรชินี	hèt phor chí nee
russula	เห็ดตะไค	hèt dtà khai
fly agaric	เห็ดพิษหมวกแดง	hèt phít mùak daeng
death cap	เห็ดระโงกหิน	hèt rá ngôhk hĭn

flower	ดอกไม้	dòrk máai
bouquet (of flowers)	ช่อดอกไม้	chôr dòrk máai
rose (flower)	ดอกกุหลาบ	dòrk gù làap
tulip	ดอกทิวลิป	dòrk thiw-líp
carnation	ดอกคาร์เนชั่น	dòrk khaa-nay-chân

camomile	ดอกคาโมมายล์	dòrk khaa-moh maai
cactus	ตะบองเพชร	dtà-bong-phét
lily of the valley	ดอกลิลลี่แหง	dòrk lí-lá-lêe hàeng
	หุบเขา	hùp khăo

| snowdrop | ดอกหยาดหิมะ | dòrk yàat hì-má |
| water lily | บัว | bua |

conservatory (greenhouse)	เรือนกระจก	reuan grà-jòk
lawn	สนามหญ้า	sà-nǎam yâa
flowerbed	สนามดอกไม้	sà-nǎam-dòrk-máai

plant	พืช	phêut
grass	หญ้า	yâa
leaf	ใบไม้	bai máai
petal	กลีบดอก	glèep dòrk
stem	ลำต้น	lam dtôn
young plant (shoot)	ต้นอ่อน	dtôn òrn

cereal crops	ธัญพืช	than-yá-phêut
wheat	ข้าวสาลี	khâao sǎa-lee
rye	ข้าวไรย์	khâao rai
oats	ข้าวโอต	khâao óht

millet	ข้าวฟ่าง	khâao fâang
barley	ข้าวบาร์เลย์	khâao baa-lây
corn	ข้าวโพด	khâao-phôht
rice	ข้าว	khâao

25. Various useful words

balance (of situation)	สมดุล	sà-má-dun
base (basis)	ฐาน	thǎan
beginning	จุดเริ่มต้น	jùt rêrm-dtôn
category	หมวดหมู่	mùat mòo

choice	ตัวเลือก	dtua lêuak
coincidence	ความบังเอิญ	khwaam bang-ern
comparison	การเปรียบเทียบ	gaan bprìap thîap
degree (extent, amount)	ระดับ	rá-dàp

development	การพัฒนา	gaan phát-thá-naa
difference	ความแตกต่าง	khwaam dtàek dtàang
effect (e.g., of drugs)	ผลกระทบ	phǒn grà-thóp
effort (exertion)	ความพยายาม	khwaam phá-yaa-yaam

element	องค์ประกอบ	ong bpra-gòrp
example (illustration)	ตัวอย่าง	dtua yàang
fact	ข้อเท็จจริง	khôr thét jing
help	ความช่วยเหลือ	khwaam chûay lěua

ideal	อุดมคติ	u-dom khá-dtì
kind (sort, type)	ประเภท	bprà-phâyt
mistake, error	ข้อผิดพลาด	khôr phìt phlâat
moment	ช่วงเวลา	chûang way-laa

obstacle	อุปสรรค	u-bpà-sàk
part (~ of sth)	ส่วน	sùan
pause (break)	การหยุดพัก	gaan yùt phák
position	ตำแหน่ง	dtam-nàeng

problem	ปัญหา	bpan-hǎa
process	กระบวนการ	grà-buan gaan
progress	ความก้าวหน้า	khwaam gâao nâa
property (quality)	คุณสมบัติ	khun-ná-sǒm-bàt

reaction	ปฏิกิริยา	bpà-dtì gì-rí-yaa
risk	ความเสี่ยง	khwaam sìang
secret	ความลับ	khwaam láp
series	ลำดับ	lam-dàp

shape (outer form)	รูปร่าง	rôop râang
situation	สถานการณ์	sà-thǎan gaan
solution	ทางแก้	thaang gâe
standard (adj)	เป็นมาตรฐาน	bpen mâat-dtrà-thǎan

stop (pause)	การหยุด	gaan yùt
style	สไตล์	sà-dtai
system	ระบบ	rá-bòp
table (chart)	ตาราง	dtaa-raang
tempo, rate	จังหวะ	jang wà

term (word, expression)	คำ	kham
truth (e.g., moment of ~)	ความจริง	khwaam jing
turn (please wait your ~)	ตา	dtaa
urgent (adj)	เร่งด่วน	râyng dùan

utility (usefulness)	ความมีประโยชน์	khwaam mee bprà-yòht
variant (alternative)	ขอ	khôr
way (means, method)	วิธีทาง	wí-thěe thaang
zone	โซน	sohn

26. Modifiers. Adjectives. Part 1

additional (adj)	เพิ่มเติม	phêrm dterm
ancient (~ civilization)	โบราณ	boh-raan
artificial (adj)	เทียม	thiam
bad (adj)	แย่	yâe
beautiful (person)	สวย	sǔay

big (in size)	ใหญ่	yài
bitter (taste)	ขม	khǒm
blind (sightless)	ตาบอด	dtaa bòrt
central (adj)	กลาง	glaang
children's (adj)	ของเด็ก	khǒrng dèk

clandestine (secret)	ลับ	láp
clean (free from dirt)	สะอาด	sà-àat
clever (smart)	ฉลาด	chà-làat
compatible (adj)	เขากันได้	khâo gan dâai
contented (satisfied)	มีความสุข	mee khwaam sùk
dangerous (adj)	อันตราย	an-dtà-raai
dead (not alive)	ตาย	dtaai
dense (fog, smoke)	หนาแน่น	năa nâen
difficult (decision)	ยาก	yâak
dirty (not clean)	สกปรก	sòk-gà-bpròk
easy (not difficult)	ง่าย	ngâai
empty (glass, room)	ว่าง	wâang
exact (amount)	ถูกต้อง	thòok dtôrng
excellent (adj)	ยอดเยี่ยม	yôrt yîam
excessive (adj)	เกินขีด	gern khèet
exterior (adj)	ภายนอก	phaai nôrk
fast (quick)	เร็ว	reo
fertile (land, soil)	อุดมสมบูรณ์	ù-dom sŏm-boon
fragile (china, glass)	เปราะบาง	bpròr baang
free (at no cost)	ฟรี	free
fresh (~ water)	จืด	jèut
frozen (food)	แช่แข็ง	châe khăeng
full (completely filled)	เต็ม	dtem
happy (adj)	มีความสุข	mee khwaam sùk
hard (not soft)	แข็ง	khăeng
huge (adj)	ใหญ่	yài
ill (sick, unwell)	ป่วย	bpùay
immobile (adj)	ไม่ขยับ	mâi khà-yàp
important (adj)	สำคัญ	săm-khan
interior (adj)	ภายใน	phaai nai
last (e.g., ~ week)	กลาย	glaai
last (final)	ท้ายสุด	tháai sùt
left (e.g., ~ side)	ซ้าย	sáai
legal (legitimate)	ทางกฎหมาย	thaang gòt măai
light (in weight)	เบา	bao
liquid (fluid)	เหลว	lĕo
long (e.g., ~ hair)	ยาว	yaao
loud (voice, etc.)	ดัง	dang
low (voice)	ต่ำ	dtàm

27. Modifiers. Adjectives. Part 2

main (principal)	หลัก	làk
matt, matte	ด้าน	dâan

mysterious (adj)	ลึกลับ	léuk láp
narrow (street, etc.)	แคบ	khâep
native (~ country)	ดั้งเดิม	dâng derm

negative (~ response)	แง่ลบ	ngâe lóp
new (adj)	ใหม่	mài
next (e.g., ~ week)	ถัดไป	thàt bpai
normal (adj)	ปกติ	bpòk-gà-dtì
not difficult (adj)	ไม่ยาก	mâi yâak

obligatory (adj)	จำเป็น	jam bpen
old (house)	เก่า	gào
open (adj)	เปิด	bpèrt
opposite (adj)	ตรงข้าม	dtrorng khâam
ordinary (usual)	ปกติ	bpòk-gà-dtì

original (unusual)	ดั้งเดิม	dâng derm
personal (adj)	ส่วนตัว	sùan dtua
polite (adj)	สุภาพ	sù-phâap
poor (not rich)	จน	jon

possible (adj)	เป็นไปได้	bpen bpai dâai
principal (main)	หลัก	làk
probable (adj)	เป็นไปได้	bpen bpai dâai
prolonged (e.g., ~ applause)	ยาวนาน	yaao naan
public (open to all)	สาธารณะ	sǎa-thaa-rá-ná

rare (adj)	หายาก	hǎa yâak
raw (uncooked)	ดิบ	dìp
right (not left)	ขวา	khwǎa
ripe (fruit)	สุก	sùk

risky (adj)	เสี่ยง	sìang
sad (~ look)	เศร้า	sâo
second hand (adj)	มือสอง	meu sǒrng
shallow (water)	ตื้น	dtêun
sharp (blade, etc.)	คม	khom

short (in length)	สั้น	sân
similar (adj)	คล้ายคลึง	khláai khleung
small (in size)	เล็ก	lék
smooth (surface)	เนียน	nian
soft (~ toys)	นิ่ม	nîm

solid (~ wall)	แข็ง	khǎeng
sour (flavor, taste)	เปรี้ยว	bprîeow
spacious (house, etc.)	กว้างขวาง	gwâang khwǎang
special (adj)	พิเศษ	phí-sàyt

| straight (line, road) | ตรง | dtrorng |
| strong (person) | แข็งแกร่ง | khǎeng gràeng |

stupid (foolish)	โง่	ngôh
superb, perfect (adj)	ยอดเยี่ยม	yôrt yîam
sweet (sugary)	หวาน	wǎan
tan (adj)	ผิวดำแดง	phǐw dam daeng
tasty (delicious)	อร่อย	à-ròi
unclear (adj)	ไม่ชัดเจน	mâi chát jayn

28. Verbs. Part 1

to accuse (vt)	กล่าวหา	glàao hǎa
to agree (say yes)	เห็นด้วย	hěn dûay
to announce (vt)	ประกาศ	bprà-gàat
to answer (vi, vt)	ตอบ	dtòrp
to apologize (vi)	ขอโทษ	khǒr thôht
to arrive (vi)	มา	maa
to ask (~ oneself)	ถาม	thǎam
to be absent	ขาด	khàat
to be afraid	กลัว	glua
to be born	เกิด	gèrt
to be in a hurry	รีบเร่ง	rêep râyng
to beat (to hit)	ตี	dtee
to begin (vt)	เริ่ม	rêrm
to believe (in God)	นับถือ	náp thěu
to belong to ...	เป็นของของ...	bpen khǒrng khǒrng...
to break (split into pieces)	แตก	dtàek
to build (vt)	สร้าง	sâang
to buy (purchase)	ซื้อ	séu
can (v aux)	สามารถ	sǎa-mâat
can (v aux)	สามารถ	sǎa-mâat
to cancel (call off)	ยกเลิก	yók lêrk
to catch (vt)	จับ	jàp
to change (vt)	เปลี่ยน	bplìan
to check (to examine)	ตรวจ	dtrùat
to choose (select)	เลือก	lêuak
to clean up (tidy)	จัดระเบียบ	jàt rá-bìap
to close (vt)	ปิด	bpìt
to compare (vt)	เปรียบเทียบ	bprìap thîap
to complain (vi, vt)	บ่น	bòn
to confirm (vt)	ยืนยัน	yeun yan
to congratulate (vt)	แสดงความยินดี	sà-daeng khwaam yin dee
to cook (dinner)	ทำอาหาร	tham aa-hǎan
to copy (vt)	คัดลอก	khát lôrk
to cost (vt)	ราคา	raa-khaa

to count (add up)	นับ	náp
to count on …	พึ่งพา	phêung phaa
to create (vt)	สร้าง	sâang
to cry (weep)	ร้องให้	rórng hâi
to dance (vi, vt)	เต้น	dtên
to deceive (vi, vt)	หลอก	lòrk
to decide (~ to do sth)	ตัดสินใจ	dtàt sĭn jai
to delete (vt)	ลบ	lóp
to demand (request firmly)	เรียกร้อง	rîak rórng
to deny (vt)	ปฏิเสธ	bpà-dtì-sàyt
to depend on …	พึ่งพา...	phêung phaa...
to despise (vt)	ดูหมิ่น	doo mìn
to die (vi)	ตาย	dtaai
to dig (vt)	ขุด	khùt
to disappear (vi)	หายตัวไป	hăai dtua bpai
to discuss (vt)	หารือ	hăa-reu
to disturb (vt)	รบกวน	róp guan

29. Verbs. Part 2

to dive (vi)	ดำน้ำ	dam náam
to divorce (vi)	หย่า	yàa
to do (vt)	ทำ	tham
to doubt (have doubts)	สงสัย	sŏng-săi
to drink (vi, vt)	ดื่ม	dèum
to drop (let fall)	ทิ้งให้ตก	thíng hâi dtòk
to dry (clothes, hair)	ทำให้...แห้ง	tham hâi...hâeng
to eat (vi, vt)	กิน	gin
to end (~ a relationship)	ยุติ	yút-dtì
to excuse (forgive)	ให้อภัย	hâi a-phai
to exist (vi)	มีอยู่	mee yòo
to expect (foresee)	คาดหวัง	khâat wăng
to explain (vt)	อธิบาย	à-thí-baai
to fall (vi)	ตก	dtòk
to fight (street fight, etc.)	สู้	sôo
to find (vt)	พบ	phóp
to finish (vt)	จบ	jòp
to fly (vi)	บิน	bin
to forbid (vt)	ห้าม	hâam
to forget (vi, vt)	ลืม	leum
to forgive (vt)	ให้อภัย	hâi a-phai
to get tired	เหนื่อย	nèuay
to give (vt)	ให้	hâi

to go (on foot)	ไป	bpai
to hate (vt)	เกลียด	glìat
to have (vt)	มี	mee
to have breakfast	ทานอาหารเช้า	thaan aa-hǎan cháo
to have dinner	ทานอาหารเย็น	thaan aa-hǎan yen
to have lunch	ทานอาหารเที่ยง	thaan aa-hǎan thîang
to hear (vt)	ได้ยิน	dâai yin
to help (vt)	ช่วย	chûay
to hide (vt)	ซ่อน	sôrn
to hope (vi, vt)	หวัง	wǎng
to hunt (vi, vt)	ล่า	lâa
to hurry (vi)	รีบ	rêep
to insist (vi, vt)	ยืนยัน	yeun yan
to insult (vt)	ดูถูก	doo thòok
to invite (vt)	เชิญ	chern
to joke (vi)	ล้อเล่น	lór lên
to keep (vt)	รักษา	rák-sǎa
to kill (vt)	ฆ่า	khâa
to know (sb)	รู้จัก	róo jàk
to know (sth)	รู้	róo
to like (I like …)	ชอบ	chôrp
to look at …	ดู	doo
to lose (umbrella, etc.)	ทำหาย	tham hǎai
to love (sb)	รัก	rák
to make a mistake	ทำผิด	tham phìt
to meet (vi, vt)	พบ	phóp
to miss (school, etc.)	พลาด	phlâat

30. Verbs. Part 3

to obey (vi, vt)	เชื่อฟัง	chêua fang
to open (vt)	เปิด	bpèrt
to participate (vi)	มีส่วนร่วม	mee sùan rûam
to pay (vi, vt)	จ่าย	jàai
to permit (vt)	อนุญาต	a-nú-yâat
to play (children)	เล่น	lên
to pray (vi, vt)	ภาวนา	phaa-wá-naa
to promise (vt)	สัญญา	sǎn-yaa
to propose (vt)	เสนอ	sà-něr
to prove (vt)	พิสูจน์	phí-sòot
to read (vi, vt)	อ่าน	àan
to receive (vt)	รับ	ráp
to rent (sth from sb)	เช่า	châo

to repeat (say again)	ซ้ำ	sám
to reserve, to book	จอง	jorng
to run (vi)	วิ่ง	wîng
to save (rescue)	กู้	gôo
to say (~ thank you)	บอก	bòrk
to see (vt)	เห็น	hěn
to sell (vt)	ขาย	khǎai
to send (vt)	ส่ง	sòng
to shoot (vi)	ยิง	ying
to shout (vi)	ตะโกน	dtà-gohn
to show (vt)	แสดง	sà-daeng
to sign (document)	ลงนาม	long naam
to sing (vi)	ร้องเพลง	rórng phlayng
to sit down (vi)	นั่ง	nâng
to smile (vi)	ยิ้ม	yím
to speak (vi, vt)	พูด	phôot
to steal (money, etc.)	ขโมย	khà-moi
to stop (please ~ calling me)	หยุด	yùt
to study (vt)	เรียน	rian
to swim (vi)	ว่ายน้ำ	wâai náam
to take (vt)	เอา	ao
to talk to …	คุยกับ	khui gàp
to tell (story, joke)	เล่า	lâo
to thank (vt)	แสดงความ ขอบคุณ	sà-daeng khwaam khòrp kun
to think (vi, vt)	คิด	khít
to translate (vt)	แปล	bplae
to trust (vt)	เชื่อ	chêua
to try (attempt)	พยายาม	phá-yaa-yaam
to turn (e.g., ~ left)	เลี้ยว	líeow
to turn off	ปิด	bpìt
to turn on	เปิด	bpèrt
to understand (vt)	เข้าใจ	khâo jai
to wait (vt)	รอ	ror
to want (wish, desire)	ต้องการ	dtôrng gaan
to work (vi)	ทำงาน	tham ngaan
to write (vt)	เขียน	khǐan

www.ingramcontent.com/pod-product-compliance
Lightning Source LLC
Chambersburg PA
CBHW060023050426
42448CB00012B/2849

* 9 7 8 1 8 3 9 5 5 0 8 1 2 *